The Stockpot and Steamer Cookbook

THE STOCKPOT

AND STEAMER COOKBOOK

by *Alice Devine Loebel*

Illustrations by VLADIMIR F. HERVERT

THE MACMILLAN COMPANY

COLLIER-MACMILLAN LTD., London

Acknowledgments

To ALL OF THE PEOPLE who assisted, tasted, criticized and praised, and who generously gave me many of their family recipes, and especially to my friends and teachers, Mrs. Anne Roe Robbins, for her warm encouragement and counsel, and Mrs. Dionne Lucas, who inspired me with the magic of food and its preparation.

A special acknowledgment to my husband, whose steadfast encouragement of, and deep interest in, my writing of this book enabled me to complete it.

And a sincere word of praise and thanks to my editor, Mr. Richard Marek, who made this labor of love a reality.

A. D. L.

Contents

Introduction

"Stock is everything in cooking. . . . Without it, nothing can be done. If one's stock is good, what remains of the work is easy; if, on the other hand, it is bad or merely mediocre, it is quite hopeless to expect anything approaching a satisfactory result."

—ESCOFFIER

THE STOCKPOT

EONS HAVE PASSED since the caveman shaped a clay pot with his hands, filled it with raw meat, bones, a few grasses and water and hung it on a stick over his fire. This ingenious man invented the stockpot.

And his method of cooking has not changed over the centuries. It is a slow simmering of meat, bones and vegetables in water with herbs and seasonings added for flavor.

During the era of large wood- and coal-burning kitchen stoves, whether in a palace or a peasant's hut, the stockpot stood permanently and majestically on back of every stove. It simmered continuously, and the savory leftovers of meals and cooking scraps were always being added. (The stockpot was probably started afresh every month or two.) If, for example, a boiled chicken, or a piece of meat, and vegetables was to be the family's dinner, the pot was pulled forward to a higher heat area of the stove and the ingredients were put into the pot. When they were cooked and removed, the pot was returned to the back of the stove. The meal was enhanced by being cooked in stock, and the next day's soup, or stew, was enriched by the meat and vegetables. A continuous cycle! Or, as Alexandre Dumas called it, "the eternal kettle."

It is my opinion that the preparation and use of homemade stocks should become as essential a part of our present-day cooking as it was for the woman in the peasant's hut or for the chef in the king's kitchen.

Stocks, like so many other foods, were brought to the peak of their refinement by the French. In French cooking each classic dish or sauce had its corresponding stock. A classic stock is made from a specific combination of ingredients.

The work to prepare all the classic stocks would be gargantuan, and freezer space to store them would be prohibitive. This book, therefore, is concerned with the making of a basic stock that is a combination of various ingredients including meats, poultry and leftovers.

The purist may shudder, but it is my experience from years of cooking and testing, that basic stock can be substituted for any of the classic meat stocks in practically all recipes. Fish stock, of course, has no substitute. Recipes for the classic stocks are included for your reference, and each recipe notes which classic stock may be used in place of the basic stock.

The use of basic stock will enable you 1) to cook more economically, 2) to cook more nutritiously, 3) to add special flavor to your cooking, 4) to save time and 5) to enjoy new recipes:

1) *Economy:* The ingredients for making a stock include the less expensive cuts of meat, bones with their rich marrow, chicken wings and necks, vegetables a bit too old, tasty leftovers, carcasses of baked fowl, roast bones, roast and steak essences, vegetable waters and peelings. All of these at-hand foods go into the pot with water to cover, and the slow simmering extracts and blends the flavors to make a delicious stock.

2) *Nutrition:* The long simmering of the ingredients extracts all the nutriments that otherwise would be discarded. For example, wine or lemon juice added to the pot extracts calcium from

the bones. Also, and extremely important today, stock is fat free. After the stock has cooked, been strained and chilled, the fat congeals on the surface and is quickly and easily removed—a blessing for everyone!

3) *Flavor:* The succulent juices of all the food in the pot are, by many hours of slow cooking, absorbed into the stock. The taste of soups, stews and sauces is enriched when they are prepared with this flavorful stock. If basic stock is added to frozen foods, dehydrated foods and canned foods, instead of water, their flavor will be improved a hundredfold.

4) *Time Saving:* An ample quantity of basic stock in the freezer will lighten the chores of daily cooking for a month or two, and delicious soups, stews or sauces can be rapidly prepared with it. But, do not be misled: There is no quick method of bypassing the work involved in the preparation and completion of basic stock. However, this work is far less arduous than cooking one truly good soup, stew or sauce without it.

Freezers have eliminated the continuous cooking of stocks because table and cooking scraps, vegetable waters and peelings can be frozen in plastic containers until the day you are ready to cook your supply of stock. Also, completed stock can be frozen for an indefinite period. Defrosting stock takes only a moment because it can be placed over direct heat. Perhaps we can update Dumas' phrase to "the eternal freezer."

5) *New Recipes:* It would be foolhardy to claim that the basic stock is a new recipe when, actually, it is a robust descendant of the stock cooked by the caveman with his first pot. However, I can claim that the use of basic stock in your favorite recipes will give them a new dash and taste.

I hope that many of the recipes in this book will be new for you. However, a recipe is a legend, and if it is researched back through time it will be found to have come from someone's great-grandmother's mother or beyond. Cooking procedures and methods change. Modern appliances have displaced hours of backbreaking grinding, chopping, mixing and fire tending. Home freezers have displaced canning, continual reheating and the simmering of the stockpot. In the near future, infrared stoves will revolutionize home cooking methods, and developments in cryogenics will make flash freezing by liquid nitrogen a daily procedure in every home.

There will be new ways to cook and freeze a stock, but the fundamental recipe will not change.

Upon completion of your first pot of stock, try one or two of the soup recipes. I have purposely included more recipes for soup than anything else because they will give you and your family an immediate appreciation and enjoyment of stocks. And when you find out how good they are, your family's fare will include, I am sure, many more delectable and nutritious soups than in your prestock days.

The only equipment needed for stockpot cooking is 1) a large pot with a capacity of six to ten quarts, and 2) freezer space. It is as easy to cook six quarts of stock as two, but you must have freezer space for storage.

Today there are stockpots of copper, stainless steel, cast iron, aluminum and enamelware ranging in capacity from one quart to many gallons. The ideal pot is heavy, and the lid should fit securely but lightly on top to permit a small amount of steam to escape. A few chefs are of the opinion that a stock made in a ceramic pot is superior to one made in a metal pot. I do not find this so, but if you are curious, make the comparison in your kitchen. Remember, the ceramic pot must have an asbestos plate between it and the heat.

THE STEAMER

Your stockpot will be used for numerous top-of-the-stove recipes, but do not overlook another marvelous use: it can be converted into a perfect steamer by adding a rack, trivet or steam basket. The age-old culinary art of steaming is exquisitely simple, tasteful and healthful. Recipes for steaming poultry, meats, fish, vegetables and desserts are included in this book, as well as explicit steaming directions. The double boiler is not a steamer, because it does not allow the steam to flow freely around the food or a mold.

The steaming of poultry, meats and vegetables over stock can be compared to a friendship: it is a give and take. The subtle flavors in the steam of the stock are absorbed into the food, and the food returns the compliment by adding some of its flavor to the stock. When the cooking is finished, the stock's volume has been decreased and this, together with the added flavor, makes an especially rich and delicious basic stock.

If your stockpot is in use and you want to steam some food, an efficient steamer can be made from any large pot, even a roasting pan, if it has a secure-fitting lid. By the way, the roasting pan is excellent for steaming a whole fish.

Steaming a dessert in a decorative metal mold, or a lard or coffee can, was an everyday affair during the era when extra fuel had to be added to the fire to heat the oven. But today, it has become rather uncommon. Steamed desserts should be gracing more tables because they are so simple to prepare, and I have found that if you cook to please a man, a steamed pudding brings him a contentment that all the glistening gelatins, frozen ices and oversweet cakes never do.

If you find the steamed recipes as delicious as I do, you may have the added enjoyment of searching for metal molds. Classic pudding molds of many shapes and sizes are available in various stores, and wonderful old metal pudding molds can often be discovered at thrift shops and secondhand stores. If the shape is attractive and there are no breaks in the metal, do not worry about the tarnish and dismal appearance of a mold. It is relatively inexpensive to have one retinned. After a tin bath, the mold emerges sparkling, decorative and ready for your use.

It is my hope that the use of the stockpot and steamer will become a pleasant habit and that they will add new dimensions to your cooking skills.

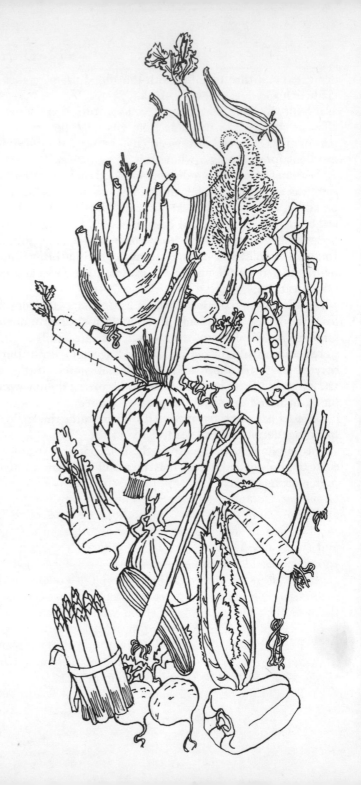

1 Stocks

STOCK NOTES

Ingredients: The ingredients given for the stock recipes should be considered as guides. To each, except the fish stock, you may add a variety of vegetables in season, such as radish tops, fresh peapods, artichokes, etc. Also, as you gain confidence in stock preparation you may wish to omit or add ingredients to your taste. I hope you will experiment.

Frozen vegetables may be added in place of fresh, but it is, of course, much more economical to use vegetables in season. The use of stocks, besides adding to the flavor of your meals, should be a saving for the family purse, not a luxury!

Because the stocks will be used to prepare many different dishes they should not be highly seasoned.

Skimming: The question of whether "to skim or not to skim" a stock while it is cooking has provoked me to considerable experimenting and has led me into the study of nutrition. My conclusion is: Do not skim. If you do not skim, you will see sediment at the bottom of the stockpot when the stock has cooled. This sediment is rich in nutriments, and it is absorbed into stews, soups and sauces and, I believe, adds to the flavor. If you need a sparkling consommé, golden broth, aspic or clear stock for a delicate sauce, clarify the stock by following the directions given later in the book.

Straining: Straining a large pot of stock may pose a problem for the beginner. The following method works efficiently for me:

1) Remove any large pieces of meat with a fork or tongs.

2) Remove all large bones with tongs or a slotted spoon.

3) Set the marrow bones aside. The marrow should be served as a food or saved to be added to a soup or stew.

4) Discard the rest of the bones.

5) Place a large strainer over a 2-quart heatproof or metal mixing bowl.

6) Place a colander over a pie plate.

7) Ladle the stock into the strainer. When the bowl is full, pour the strained stock into containers and dump the pulpy ingredients into the colander.

8) Continue straining and dumping until the pot is empty.

9) Leave the pulpy mass of ingredients in the colander to drain. Press it with the back of a large spoon to squeeze out all the stock. Add this liquid to the containers and discard the pulp.

Freezing: Remove all fat from the stock and freeze at least a quart of the stock in an ice tray. When it is frozen, put the cubes into a plastic bag and back into the freezer. When you need a small amount of stock for braising or to add to a sauce, use 1 or 2 cubes. Each cube is approximately 2 tablespoons.

This is the basic stock recipe and, as previously stated, I believe it is the stock to use in all recipes except, of course, the fish recipes. In each recipe I have given the individual, classic stocks used in French haute cuisine, but the basic stock may be substituted with no loss of quality in the recipes.

Prepare in advance to make your basic stock by freezing in plastic bags or containers all the leftover meat and bones of beef, veal and lamb roasts, steak bones and meat scraps, and the carcasses of roasted chickens, turkeys, ducks and game birds. Do not use the bone or meat of ham or pork. These should be saved to use in the classic ham stock.

Freeze the drippings from the roasting pan and broiler. To obtain these drippings place the roasting pan or broiler on top of the stove, add a small quantity of water or wine and bring to a fast boil; rapidly scrape all the brown crusts from the pan and pour the liquid and crusts into a container and freeze.

If freezer space is available, freeze the water in which vegetables have been steamed or boiled. Do not use the water from beets, cauliflower, parsnips or cabbage. And if you are really vitamin conscious, freeze the peelings of carrots, tomatoes, turnips, as well as the large tough stems of asparagus, parsley and watercress. Add any or all of them to the pot.

When your savory meat and bone scraps total around two or three pounds you are ready to start your first pot of basic stock.

§ BASIC STOCK

2 to 3 lbs. various meat and bone scraps and meat leftovers

2 to 3 lbs. chicken necks and wings

4 beef marrow bones, cut into 4-inch pieces

1 veal knuckle, cracked

6 medium carrots, washed and cut into 2-inch pieces

2 large onions, peeled and studded with 4 cloves

4 medium leeks, washed and cut into 2-inch pieces, including the fresh green tops

2 medium white turnips, washed and quartered

4 cloves garlic, peeled

2 bay leaves

6 tbs. salt

16 peppercorns

6 stalks celery, including the leaves, washed and cut into 2-inch pieces

8 sprigs parsley

1 cup of red or dry white wine

Vegetable waters

Cold water

Crack any large roast bones with a cleaver.

Put all the ingredients into an 8- to 10-quart soup pot. Add cold water to cover by 2 inches. Place a loose-fitting lid on top and bring slowly to a boil. Immediately adjust the heat so that the stock simmers lazily. Stir occasionally. Simmer 4 to 5 hours. Turn off the heat and cool.

When cool, strain the stock into containers and refrigerate. When cold, remove and discard all the fat congealed on the surface of the stock. Refrigerate the stock for immediate use, or place in the freezer for future use.

This recipe makes 5 to 6 quarts.

Variations:

a) Add 1 3- to 4-lb. chicken. Remove after 1 hour of cooking, or when tender.

b) Add 3 lbs. brisket of beef. Remove after 2 hours of cooking.

c) Add 1 lb. chicken giblets.

d) Add 2 lbs. short ribs of beef.

e) Add 2 cups canned or fresh tomatoes, with 2 tsp. sugar.

f) Add the juice of 1 lemon instead of the wine.

g) Add 1 head of lettuce washed and coarsely sliced.

h) Add ¼ lb. fresh or frozen mushrooms or mushroom stems.

i) For a stronger stock remove the lid during the last hour of cooking and turn up the heat so that the pot boils gently.

§ CLASSIC CHICKEN STOCK

1 4-lb. chicken or a 5-lb. fowl
2½ lbs. chicken necks and wings
1 veal knuckle, cracked
1 medium onion, stuck with 3 cloves
4 medium carrots, washed and cut into quarters
2 medium leeks, washed and cut into 1-inch pieces, including the fresh green leaves

2 stalks celery, washed, including leaves, cut into 1-inch pieces
½ tsp. thyme
1 bay leaf
1 clove garlic, peeled
2 tbs. salt
6 peppercorns
3 sprigs parsley
1 cup dry white wine
Cold water

Place all the ingredients into a large 8- to 10-quart soup pot. Add cold water to cover by 2 inches. Place a loose-fitting lid on top and bring slowly to a boil. Immediately adjust heat to a simmer, and simmer for 3 to 4 hours. Turn off the heat and cool.

When cool, strain all the stock into containers and refrigerate. When cold, remove and discard all the fat congealed on the surface of the stock. Refrigerate the stock for same day use, or freeze for future use.

This recipe makes approximately 4 quarts.

Variations:

a) Omit the veal knuckle.

b) Add 2 lbs. lean veal.

c) Add 1 3-lb. chicken and remove after 1 hour of cooking, or when tender. This chicken can be served at once, or the meat used for a chicken salad or a chicken casserole.

d) Add 2 tbs. lemon juice instead of the wine.

e) Add 1 lb. chicken gizzards and hearts.

f) Add 1 cup canned tomatoes with 1 teaspoon sugar.

g) Add 2 small white turnips, washed and halved.

h) Add ¼-lb. fresh mushrooms or mushroom stems.

i) Add 4 chicken feet. Before adding to the pot, prepare them as follows: Place in a pan, cover with cold water and bring to a boil. Remove and plunge them into cold water. Remove and discard the scaly yellow outer skin.

j) Add the carcass of a roasted chicken.

k) For a stronger stock remove the lid during the last hour of cooking and turn up the heat so that the pot boils gently.

Note: The meat from the large chicken or fowl may be used in making chicken croquettes.

§ CLASSIC BEEF STOCK

½ cup dried mushrooms
2 lbs. short ribs of beef
2 lbs. beef marrow bones, cut into 2- to 4-inch pieces
1 veal knuckle, cracked
1 lb. ground beef chuck
1 large onion, peeled and coarsely chopped
1 clove garlic, peeled
3 medium carrots, washed and cut into quarters

2 tbs. salt
10 peppercorns
1 bay leaf
1 tsp. mace
1 tsp. thyme
3 sprigs parsley
3 ribs celery, including leaves, washed and quartered
1 cup dry red wine
1 tbs. soy sauce
Cold water

Soak the dried mushrooms in 1 cup of warm water for 15 minutes.

Put all the ingredients into a 6- to 8-quart soup pot including the water in which the mushrooms were soaked. Cover with cold water by 2 inches. Place a loose-fitting lid on top, bring to a boil. Immediately adjust heat to a simmer, and simmer for 3 to 4 hours. Turn off the heat and cool.

When cool, strain all the stock into containers and refrigerate. When cold, remove and discard all the fat congealed on the surface. Refrigerate the stock for immediate use, or freeze for future use.

This recipe makes approximately 3½ quarts.

Variations:

a) Add 3 lbs. brisket of beef. Remove after 2 hours of cooking.

b) Add 1 cup of canned or fresh tomatoes, with 1 tsp. sugar.

c) Add 2 tbs. of lemon juice instead of the wine.

d) Add any roast beef or steak drippings.

e) Add any roast beef or steak bones.

f) For a stronger stock remove the lid during the last hour of cooking and turn up the heat so that the pot boils gently.

§ *CLASSIC BROWN STOCK*

4½ lbs. beef bones, including at least 4 marrow bones

3 lbs. veal bones, including 1 knuckle

1 medium onion, peeled and coarsely sliced

1 medium carrot, washed and quartered

1 cup dry red wine or water

Have your butcher crack and saw the bones into 2- to 4-inch pieces.

Put the bones, onion and carrot into a large roasting pan. Place in a 400° F. oven for 45 to 50 minutes. Occasionally turn the bones so that they brown evenly on all sides.

Remove pan from the oven and put the bones into a 8- to 10-quart soup pot. Deglaze the roasting pan with the wine or water and add to the pot. Also add:

2 medium carrots, washed and quartered
2 medium leeks, including the fresh green leaves, washed and cut into coarse slices
1 large onion, peeled and quartered
4 stalks celery, washed and quartered
1 bay leaf
3 tbs. salt
10 peppercorns
1 cup canned tomatoes
1 tbs. tomato paste
1 tsp. sugar
1 cup dry red wine
Cold water to cover the ingredients by 1 inch

Bring to a boil. Adjust heat to a simmer, cover with a loose-fitting lid and simmer 4 to 5 hours. Turn off the heat and cool.

When cool, strain into containers and refrigerate. When cold, remove and discard all the fat congealed on the surface of the stock. Refrigerate the stock for immediate use, or place in the freezer for future use.

This recipe makes approximately 6 quarts.

Variations:

a) Add the carcass of a roast chicken.
b) Add 3 lbs. brisket of beef. Remove after 2 hours of cooking.
c) Add any roast beef or steak drippings.
d) Add any steak or roast beef bones.
e) Add 2 tbs. of lemon juice instead of the wine.
f) For a stronger stock remove the lid during the last hour of cooking and turn up the heat so that the pot boils gently.

§ CLASSIC VEAL STOCK

3 to 4 lbs. veal knuckles, cracked
1 lb. shoulder, neck or shin of veal, cubed
1 cup dry white wine
1 tbs. salt
8 peppercorns
2 medium leeks, including the fresh green leaves, washed and cut into 2-inch pieces
1 medium onion, peeled and stuck with 2 cloves
1 clove garlic, peeled
2 stalks celery, including leaves, washed and quartered
2 medium carrots, washed and quartered
1 bay leaf
4 sprigs parsley
Cold water

Put all the ingredients into a large soup pot. Add water to cover by 1 inch. Bring slowly to a boil, place a loose-fitting lid on top and adjust the heat to a simmer. Simmer for 3 to 4 hours. Turn off the heat and cool.

When cool, strain into containers and refrigerate. When cold, remove and discard all the fat congealed on the surface of the stock. Refrigerate the stock for immediate use, or freeze for future use.

This recipe makes approximately 3 quarts.

Variations:

a) Add 1 3½-lb. chicken and remove after 1 hour of cooking or when tender.

b) Add the carcass of a roasted chicken.

c) Add 1 small white turnip, washed and halved.

d) Add 2 tbs. lemon juice instead of the wine.

§ CLASSIC HAM STOCK

No salt measurement is given, because the ham may season the stock sufficiently. If not, add salt to taste.

1 ham bone	4 stalks celery, including leaves, washed and quartered
4 quarts cold water	1 clove garlic, peeled
1 cup dry white wine	½ tsp. thyme
1 large onion, peeled and quartered	7 peppercorns
2 medium carrots, scrubbed and quartered	1 bay leaf
	3 sprigs parsley

If the ham bone is large, crack and break it with a cleaver.

Put all the ingredients into a large pot and bring slowly to a boil. Immediately adjust the heat to a simmer, cover with a loose-fitting lid and simmer for 2 to 3 hours. Turn off the heat and cool.

When cool, strain the stock and pour into containers. Save the small pieces of ham to add to a soup. Refrigerate the stock. When cold, remove and discard all the fat congealed on the surface of the stock. Refrigerate the stock for immediate use, or store in the freezer for future use.

This recipe makes approximately 3 quarts.

Variations:

a) Add any pork roast bones or pork meat scraps.
b) Add any pieces of bacon rind.
c) Add 2 tbs. of lemon juice instead of the wine.

§ FISH STOCK

This is quick and simple to prepare. I suggest it be prepared in small quantities so that valuable freezer space can be saved for more complicated stocks. However, it is convenient to have a few cups on hand for a fish sauce or soup or for cooking rice to accompany a fish dish.

I recommend using flounder, halibut or whiting. Frozen fish can be used, but the stock will have more flavor if the head, tail and backbone of a fresh fish are added to the pot.

1½ lbs. fresh or frozen fish	2 sprigs parsley
1 medium onion, peeled and finely chopped	3 slices lemon
	8 peppercorns
2 ribs of celery, cut into small pieces	2 tsps. salt
	¾ cup dry white wine
1 medium carrot, scrubbed and finely diced	3 cups cold water

Put all the ingredients into a pot and bring slowly to a boil. Cover with a loose-fitting lid. Immediately adjust the heat to a simmer, and simmer for 30 minutes. Turn off the heat and cool.

When cool, strain through a fine sieve into a container. Refrigerate the stock if it is to be used within a day or two. If not, store in the freezer for future use.

This makes approximately 3½ cups of stock.

§ TO CLARIFY STOCK

For a sparkling-clear stock for preparing aspics and special sauces, the following method is used:

4 cups cold stock   1 egg shell
2 egg whites

Remove every particle of fat from the stock and check that there is no grease in the pot. Pour the cold stock into the pot. Lightly beat the egg whites with a fork or wire whisk and crush the egg shell.

Place the pot over medium heat, pour the egg whites into the stock, add the egg shell and beat with a whisk until the liquid begins to boil. Stop beating but watch the pot carefully. Turn heat off at once as the stock comes up to a hard boil. Remove the pot from the stove and set aside. Do not disturb for at least 15 minutes.

Pour gently into a container through a fine strainer lined with 2 layers of cheesecloth wrung out in cold water. The cold cloth traps any particle of fat that might have lingered in the stock.

2 Soups

SOUP NOTES

FROZEN VEGETABLES may be used instead of fresh vegetables in making soups. The cost is greater, but the time saved may make their use worth your while.

Canned broth may be used instead of your own stock, but a lot of flavor will be forfeited.

All soups, except the cold soups, should be served piping hot in heated bowls or tureens.

All pepper should be freshly ground peppercorns.

Taste before you serve! Correct the seasoning to *your* taste.

§ BEEF CONSOMMÉ

The difference between clarified stock and consommé is that the stock used to make the consommé is strengthened by the addition of meat and vegetables and by simmering it uncovered to reduce its volume.

Consommé may be served plain or with any of numerous garnishes added. Consommé is the base for a few soups, but it is not used in sauces or stews.

10 cups cold basic stock, beef stock or brown stock from which all fat has been removed
½ lb. lean ground beef
1 medium carrot, scrubbed and sliced in thin rounds
1 leek, or 3 scallions, including the fresh green leaves, washed and thinly sliced
1 stalk celery, washed and finely diced
1 tsp. salt
3 peppercorns
2 egg whites

Put all the ingredients into a large pot. Slowly bring to a boil, beating continuously with a whisk or fork. When the mixture comes to a boil, immediately lower the heat to a simmer. Simmer uncovered for 1 to 1½ hours. Set aside to cool.

Line a fine strainer with 2 layers of cheesecloth wrung out in cold water, and when the consommé is cool, strain it into a container.

To serve: Heat and serve in individual heated cups, or add any one of the vegetable garnishes listed or a garnish to suit your taste.

This recipe makes 7 to 8 cups.

Note: If all the fat has been removed from the stock, if the beef is lean and if the cheesecloth is wrung out in cold water, there should be no fat in the consommé. Should fat be present, chill the consommé and discard any fat congealed on the surface.

Vegetable Garnishes:

The following vegetables should be added to hot consommé, covered and simmered for 5 minutes. Allow 1 to 2 tablespoons of vegetables per serving.

Carrots: Peeled and cut into julienne strips or paper-thin rounds or finely diced.

Celery: Washed and cut into 2-inch julienne strips or diced into tiny squares.

Leeks: Washed and the white part cut into julienne strips or thin rounds.

Turnips: Peeled and cut into julienne strips or finely diced.

The following vegetables should be stirred into the boiling consommé at the last moment. Heat, but do not cook. Serve at once. Except where otherwise specified, allow 1 to 2 teaspoons per serving.

Carrots: Peeled and finely grated.

Celery: Leaves washed and finely chopped.

Scallions: Washed and cut into paper-thin round slices, including the fresh green tops, or finely chopped.

Tomatoes: Peeled, seeded and cut into julienne strips or finely diced.

Spinach: Leaves sliced into julienne strips.

Watercress: Small whole tender leaves.

Mushrooms: Cleaned and finely chopped. 1 small mushroom per serving.

Ginger root: Peeled and cut. 1 or 2 paper-thin rounds per serving.

Escarole: 1 or 2 leaves washed and finely shredded.

Parsley: Finely chopped.

Chives: Finely chopped.

§ CHICKEN CONSOMMÉ

10 cups cold chicken stock from which all fat has been removed
1 lb. chicken necks and wings
1 medium carrot, scrubbed and sliced in thin rounds

1 leek, or 3 scallions, including the fresh green leaves, washed and thinly sliced
1 stalk celery, washed and finely diced
1 tsp. salt
3 peppercorns
2 egg whites

Put all the ingredients into a large pot. Slowly bring to a boil, beating continuously with a whisk or fork. When the mixture comes to a boil, immediately lower the heat to a simmer. Simmer uncovered for 1 to 1½ hours. Set aside to cool.

Line a fine strainer with 2 layers of cheesecloth wrung out in cold water, and when the consommé is cool strain it into a container.

To serve: Heat and serve in individual heated cups, or add any one of the vegetable garnishes listed for beef consommé.

This makes approximately 2 quarts.

Variations:

a) Add 1 3-lb. chicken. Remove after 1 hour of cooking, or when tender.

b) Add 1 lb. chicken gizzards and hearts.

§ JELLIED CONSOMMÉ

If the preceding beef or chicken consommé recipe has been followed, this consommé should be jelled when it is cold. A small amount of gelatin is added to insure that it does not melt at the edges during serving or eating.

2 tsps. unflavored gelatin
4 tbs. cold beef or chicken consommé
4 cups beef or chicken consommé

¼ tsp. salt
¼ cup Madeira
Lemon wedges

Dissolve the gelatin in the cold consommé.

Pour the 4 cups of consommé into a pot and bring to a boil. Add the gelatin and stir until it is completely dissolved. Add the salt and Madeira. Stir and pour into a container, cover and refrigerate until set, approximately 1 to 3 hours.

To serve: Spoon into small chilled bowls and garnish with the lemon wedges.

Serves 6.

Variation: Remove the seed and fill the center of half an avocado with the jellied consommé, add a squeeze of lemon juice and serve it as a first course. Allow half an avocado per serving.

§ EGG RIBBON CONSOMMÉ

6 cups beef or chicken con-
    sommé
2 tsps. soy sauce

4 scallions, including the fresh
    green leaves, finely chopped
2 eggs

Put the consommé into a pot, add soy sauce and scallions. Bring to a boil.

Beat the eggs lightly. When the stock boils, stir it rapidly with a long-handled wooden spoon to make a whirlpool in the center of the pot. With the other hand hold the bowl of eggs high up and slowly pour, stirring continuously, into the consommé. The eggs, when cooked, are long, thin ribbon strips. Serve in heated consommé bowls or cups.

Serves 6.

§ PANCAKE CONSOMMÉ

These thin, tender pancakes turn any stock into an important soup. Men particularly enjoy this soup. Because the pancake slices can be frozen, the soup can be prepared effortlessly.

½ cup sifted flour
2 eggs
2 egg yolks
½ tsp. salt
¼ cup vegetable oil

1 cup milk
Butter
2 quarts beef or chicken con-
    sommé

Put the flour, eggs, egg yolks, salt and vegetable oil into a bowl and mix. Add the milk and beat until thoroughly blended. Pour into a container with a tight-fitting lid and refrigerate for 1 or 2 hours. The batter improves if it is stored in the refrigerator for 2 or 3 days.

Place a skillet, 8½ inches in diameter, over the heat. Stir or shake up the batter. Using a rolled-up stick of wax paper, pick up a small dab of softened butter and rub it around the sides and bottom of the skillet. When the skillet is piping hot, pour 3 tablespoons of the batter into it, and tilt and turn the pan so that the batter covers the full bottom of the pan. Keep the heat high. When all the pancake has a shiny, waxy surface, after about 20 or 30 seconds, turn and cook the other side. Turn the pancake out on a plate. With the wax-paper stick, pick up another piece of butter, lightly dab the skillet again and continue the process until the batter is used up.

Roll the pancakes, 2 or 3 at a time, and with a sharp knife cut into strips as thin as possible. Set aside.

Bring the consommé to a boil, taste and correct the seasoning.

Place an equal amount of pancake slices into individual heated bowls, or all the slices into a heated tureen, and pour the hot consommé over them. Serve at once.

If the pancake slices are frozen, drop them into the hot consommé for barely a minute or two to thaw. Do not boil. Ladle into bowls or a tureen and serve.

From this batter you should have 12 or 14 pancakes.

Serves 6 to 8.

Variation: Add 1 tablespoon of finely chopped parsley to the pancake batter.

§ ASPIC

Aspic is not a soup, but as it is made from stock, a soup base, I have included it in the soup recipes.

Aspic is beautiful. It adds sparkle and beauty to a commonplace dish. If covered, it will keep in the refrigerator for 2 to 3 weeks. It can be frozen, defrosted over a medium direct heat and put in the refrigerator to reset and use. When finely chopped it makes an elegant garnish for simple cold cuts and cold roasts and deviled eggs, pâté and other canapés.

If you have aspic on hand, a cupful can be melted down, and "eggs in aspic" or a jelled vegetable salad can be quickly prepared. To seal in the moisture and preserve the freshness of cooked eggs, meats, and vegetables fresh or cooked, coat them with aspic; this method is centuries old but still a superb one.

Make some up without any specific use in mind. If you have it in the refrigerator, particularly during the summer, you will find many good ways to serve it.

5 cups basic stock or brown stock from which all fat has been removed
4 tbs. unflavored gelatin
½ cup cold water
3 tsps. salt

1 tsp. pepper
½ tsp. lemon juice
1 egg shell, crushed
2 tsps. soy sauce
2 egg whites, lightly beaten
2 tbs. brandy or Madeira

Put the stock into a metal pot. Be certain that the stock and the pot are completely free of any fat.

Put the gelatin into a small bowl and soften it with the cold water.

To the stock add the salt, pepper, lemon juice, egg shell, soy sauce and softened gelatin. Stir. Pour in the egg whites and place over a medium heat. Beat with a wire whisk until the liquid comes to a boil. Boil for 2 minutes. Remove the pot from the heat and leave undisturbed for at least 15 minutes.

Rinse out 2 thicknesses of cheesecloth in cold water; wring out thoroughly and place them in a strainer. Pour the aspic carefully into the strainer lined with the cheesecloth. Drain. Discard egg white and accumulated particles.

Add the brandy or Madeira to the aspic and pour into a metal bread-loaf tin. Cover and place in the refrigerator to set, 2 to 4 hours.

This makes approximately 1 quart.

§ GROG BOUILLON

This is an elegant first course, but before giving the recipe I would like to digress briefly to speak of dinner or luncheon courses.

*Every woman who enjoys cooking wants to present her accom-
plishments as attractively as possible. However, when help is un-
available, the jumping up and down to serve many courses is
nerve-racking for both hostess and guests.*

*I have worked out the following serving method when I have
guests and no help. The first course is planned to be a clear bouillon. After the time allotted for cocktails has passed, I serve the
grog bouillon, or any other clear bouillon or consommé, as follows:
The bouillon is ready and hot on the stove; the small attractive Chinese or Japanese bowls, in which it is to be served, are
warm. I fill the bowls, place them on a tray, serve each guest
in the living room, and with the same tray pick up the glasses and
canapé plates. The guests drink the bouillon from the bowls; no
serving plates or spoons are needed. The touch of the warm bowls,
the smell and the taste of an aromatic clear bouillon gently pre-
pares the senses for the dinner to follow.*

4 cinnamon sticks	5 cups clarified basic stock, or
1 tbs. sugar	clarified beef stock
2 cups claret	6 slices lemon, cut paper thin

Four to 6 hours before serving, place the cinnamon sticks, sugar
and claret in a pot. Bring to a boil and boil for 2 minutes. Place a
cover on the pot and set aside to marinate. Do not put the mixture
into the refrigerator.

When ready to serve, strain the claret mixture into the clarified
stock and heat.

To serve: Pour into warmed bowls and float a slice of lemon on
the top of each bowl.

Serves 6.

§ MUSHROOM BOUILLON

*This is a refreshing and aromatic bouillon. You may garnish it
with a thin slice of lemon in each cup, finely chopped chives or
parsley. However, I prefer it plain so that the smoky flavor of the
mushroom essence is not adulterated.*

1½ lbs. fresh mushrooms, including stems, or frozen mushrooms
½ tsp. lemon juice

4 cups clarified basic stock or
clarified chicken stock
1 tsp. salt
½ tsp. pepper
2 tbs. Madeira

Clean mushrooms and chop them coarsely. Sprinkle with the lemon juice. Put the clarified stock into a pot, add mushrooms and simmer for 30 to 40 minutes with a loose-fitting lid on top.

Remove from heat and strain through a strainer lined with 2 layers of cheesecloth. Leave the mushrooms in the cheesecloth, and with your hands twist the cheesecloth firmly so that all the juices are extracted from them.

Pour the liquid back into the pot, add salt and pepper, place over a medium heat and bring to a boil. Add Madeira.

Serve immediately in warmed cups or small bowls.

Serves 6.

§ PETITE MARMITE MARIE

Petite marmite *is the name of a French glazed ceramic pot. Many French cooks believe that the pot gives a special flavor to soups. This type of pot is not commonly used in this country, but many houseware shops sell specially imported* petite marmite *pots.*

If you have one, do serve this elegant soup from it. The soup is simple to prepare, but the broth must be crystal clear, strong in flavor, and the few garnishes neatly diced. If possible, serve it in small white or light-colored cups or bowls so that the sparkle of the broth can be admired.

10 cups basic stock or brown
stock from which all fat
has been removed
1 carrot, scrubbed and quartered
2 stalks celery, washed and
coarsely chopped
1 small onion, peeled and
coarsely chopped
1 tsp. salt
1 lb. chopped lean beef

¼ cup carrots, peeled and finely
diced
¼ cup celery stalks, finely diced
¼ cup white turnips, peeled and
finely diced
¼ cup peas
¼ cup cooked chicken breast,
finely diced
¼ cup cooked brisket of beef,
finely diced and all fat removed

Put the stock into a large pot and add the carrot, celery, onion, salt and chopped beef. Bring to a boil, adjust heat to a simmer, place a loose-fitting lid on top and simmer for 1 hour. Strain into a container. Refrigerate until all fat has congealed on the surface. Remove every speck of fat.

Clarify the stock according to instructions given on p. 15.

Put the clarified stock into a pot, bring to a boil and add the diced carrots, celery, turnips, peas, chicken breast and beef. Let simmer for 5 to 8 minutes.

Serve piping hot from a *petite marmite* pot or in heated individual bowls.

Serves 6.

§ GAZPACHO

This is a blender recipe. It is quickly prepared and can be kept in the refrigerator for at least a week. It is the perfect first course for a hot day's lunch or supper, and is delightfully refreshing as a pickup on a midsummer's afternoon. Use fully sun-ripened tomatoes.

1½ cups clarified basic, chicken or beef stock

1 medium clove garlic, peeled and halved

4 large tomatoes, peeled and quartered

½ medium green pepper, seeded and the white membranes removed, cut into thick slices

½ small onion, peeled and coarsely chopped

1 medium cucumber, peeled and coarsely sliced

1 tsp. salt

½ tsp. pepper

2 tbs. olive oil

2 tbs. wine vinegar

½ tsp. Worcestershire Sauce

1 tsp. lemon juice

½ cup chilled basic, chicken or beef stock from which all fat has been removed

Put the clarified stock into an ice cube tray and freeze.

Into the blender put the garlic, tomatoes, green pepper, onion, cucumber, salt, pepper, olive oil, vinegar, Worcestershire Sauce, lemon juice and unclarified stock. Cover and blend 3 to 6 seconds or until the vegetables are coarsely chopped. Pour into a jar and chill.

To serve: Pour into chilled bowls, and place 1 cube of frozen stock into each bowl. Serve at once.

Serves 4 to 6.

§ *CUCUMBER AND YOGURT SOUP*

Refreshing and delicious. If you try it on a summer's first hot day you'll become an addict like many others and continue to serve it up to and through winter's cold days.

3 cups plain yogurt

3 cups chilled basic stock or chicken stock from which all fat has been removed

2 tbs. olive oil

2 medium cucumbers, peeled and diced into ¼-inch cubes

3 tbs. walnuts, finely chopped

2 small cloves garlic, finely chopped

½ tsp. salt

¼ tsp. pepper

4 scallions, including the fresh green tops, washed and finely chopped

2 tsps. lemon juice

Put the yogurt and stock into a bowl and mix. Beating continuously, add the olive oil slowly to blend it thoroughly into the soup. Add the cucumbers, walnuts, garlic, salt, pepper, scallions and lemon juice. Mix well and chill.

Serve in chilled soup bowls or from a chilled tureen.

Serves 6.

Variation: Omit walnuts.

§ *ESCAROLE SOUP*

Escarole, so good in salads, is a welcome addition to the soup pot. This is an easy, delicious and economical soup.

¾ lb. lean ground beef
¼ tsp. garlic, finely chopped
3 tbs. freshly grated Parmesan
  cheese
1 egg, slightly beaten
1 tsp. salt
½ tsp. pepper
2 quarts basic stock or beef
  stock from which all fat has
  been removed
2 tbs. tomato paste

½ tsp. sugar
1 lb. escarole, washed and
  coarsely chopped
2 large onions, peeled and
  finely diced
1 cup celery stalks, washed and
  diced
2 large potatoes, peeled and cut
  into small cubes
2 tbs. parsley, finely chopped

Mix the ground beef with the garlic, cheese, egg, salt and pepper. Form into balls ½ to 1 inch in diameter. Set aside.

In a large pot pour the stock. Add the tomato paste and sugar. Bring to a boil and add meatballs. Turn heat down and simmer uncovered for 10 minutes. Add the escarole, onions, celery and potatoes. Cover with a loose-fitting lid and simmer for 30 minutes.

Serve directly from the pot or from a heated soup tureen. Garnish with the parsley.

Serves 8 to 10.

§ VICHYSSOISE (COLD POTATO AND LEEK SOUP)

Delicious, and a must for the hot summer days.

If you are pressed for time, frozen potatoes can be substituted for fresh potatoes without any loss of flavor or texture.

I recommend adding the light cream just before serving. The potato, leek and stock base keeps well in the refrigerator up to 10 days. If it is prepared in advance, one or two cups of this refreshing soup may be made ready at once. One time I left a cup of the mixture too long, and it had started to sour. Before I was able to throw it out, a friend mixed herself a cup with the sweet light cream and swears that the touch of "sourness" or fermentation improved the soup tremendously. I do not share her opinion, but I do have such a high regard for her taste that I pass the idea on to you.

1 tbs. butter
4 leeks, washed, and the white parts coarsely sliced
1 medium onion, peeled and coarsely sliced
4 cups potatoes, peeled and coarsely sliced

4 cups basic stock or chicken stock from which all fat has been removed
3 tsps. salt
½ tsp. pepper
3 cups light cream
Chives or scallions, finely chopped

In a large pot melt butter, add leeks and onion. Cook over a medium heat, stirring until leeks and onion are transparent. Do not brown. Add potatoes, stock, salt and pepper. Bring to a boil, cover with a loose-fitting lid, adjust heat to a simmer and simmer for 30 to 40 minutes or until potatoes are tender.

Put the mixture through a food mill or blend in a blender until smooth. Pour into a container, cover and chill thoroughly.

To serve: Pour the mixture into a large bowl and add cold light cream. Mix thoroughly with a whisk or beater. Pour into chilled individual soup cups or small bowls. Garnish with chives or scallions.

Serves 6 to 8.

Note: For an individual serving, combine 1 cup of potato and leek mixture with ½ cup light cream. If you prefer a thinner soup, add more light cream.

§ ASPARAGUS AND POTATO SOUP

If you are a frozen-food fan, this delicious soup can be made in a couple of minutes. However, when fresh asparagus is in season it is economically prudent to make up a generous supply and freeze it for future use.

1 bunch (approximately 2½ lbs.) fresh asparagus, or 2 packages frozen asparagus
4 cups basic stock or chicken stock from which all fat has been removed

3 medium potatoes, peeled and quartered, or an equal amount of frozen potatoes
2 tsps. salt
½ tsp. pepper
2 egg yolks
½ cup heavy cream
½ tsp. grated nutmeg

Clean the fresh asparagus, discarding the tough fiber ends, and cut into 3-inch pieces. Bring 2 cups of the stock to a boil. Add the asparagus and cook until almost tender. If frozen asparagus are used, follow the same cooking procedure. Remove the asparagus and set aside. Save a few asparagus tips for garnish.

Bring the liquid in which the asparagus were cooked back to a boil and add the potatoes. Cook until tender. When tender, put the potatoes and asparagus together with the liquid through a sieve, or blend in a blender until smooth.

Put the purée mixture into a pot, add the 2 remaining cups of stock, salt and pepper and simmer 5 to 10 minutes, stirring occasionally.

Beat the egg yolks with the cream and add very slowly to the soup, stirring continuously. Add nutmeg. Heat but do not boil.

Serve in individual heated soup bowls and garnish with the asparagus tips.

Serves 6.

Note: If the soup is frozen, defrost and heat it in a double boiler over hot water. Give it a good beating with a wire whisk from time to time.

§ POTATO AND BACON SOUP

4 tbs. butter
2 tbs. vegetable oil
6 medium potatoes, peeled and cut in small cubes
4 medium onions, peeled and thinly sliced

6 cups basic stock or brown stock from which all fat has been removed
3 tsps. salt
½ tsp. pepper
½ lb. bacon, cut into 1-inch pieces
½ cup grated Parmesan cheese

Heat butter and vegetable oil in a large, heavy pot. When hot, add potatoes. Cook 10 minutes over a medium heat, turning them often. Add onions and continue to fry until the potatoes and onions are golden brown. Add stock, salt and pepper. Bring to a boil. Place a loose-fitting lid on top, adjust heat to a simmer and simmer 30 minutes, or until potatoes are soft.

Meanwhile, fry the bacon pieces until crisp. Drain on a paper towel and crumble into fine bits.

Pour the soup into a heated tureen. Put the crumbled bacon and Parmesan cheese into two side dishes.

To serve: Ladle the soup into heated soup plates and sprinkle each with a heaping tablespoon of bacon and cheese.

Serves 6 to 8.

§ *POTATO AND SPINACH SOUP*

A soup which freezes perfectly. Sorrel leaves or watercress leaves may be substituted for the spinach. If you prepare it with watercress, use only the leaves and the tiny leaf stems; do not use the large, firm center stalk.

1 quart potatoes, peeled and diced	2 ozs. butter
1 large onion, peeled and coarsely sliced	1 tsp. salt
	½ tsp. pepper
1 quart basic stock or chicken stock from which all fat has been removed	½ lb. spinach leaves, washed
	1 cup light cream

Put the potatoes and onion in a large pot. Add stock, bring to a boil, cover with a loose-fitting lid, adjust heat to a simmer and simmer for 30 minutes or until potatoes are tender. Add butter, salt and pepper.

Turn the heat off and add spinach. Stir until spinach is wilted. Pour the mixture through a food mill, or blend in a blender until smooth. Return the mixture to the pot, add cream and heat. Do not boil.

Serve in a heated tureen or in heated individual soup bowls.

Serves 6.

§ AVOCADO SOUP

This thick soup is so rich that if you serve it as a first course, keep the portions small. If it is too thick for your taste, add a bit more stock. It is easy to prepare and freezes well.

2 tbs. butter
2 medium onions, peeled and finely chopped
3 tbs. flour
1 small clove garlic, peeled and finely chopped
2 tsps. salt
⅛ tsp. cayenne pepper
¼ tsp. ground cloves
¼ tsp. nutmeg
4 cups basic stock or chicken stock from which all fat has been removed
3 medium avocados
4 tsps. lemon juice
1 cup light cream
Croutons

Melt butter in a large, heavy pot; when foaming, add onions and cook until transparent. Remove from heat and stir in flour, garlic, salt, pepper, cloves and nutmeg. Add stock, return to heat and bring to a boil, stirring constantly. Adjust heat to a simmer and simmer for 10 minutes.

Peel the avocados and remove seeds. Dice into coarse pieces. Add to the soup, stir and cook 1 or 2 minutes. Add lemon juice.

Put the mixture through a food mill or blend in a blender until smooth. Return the mixture to the pot, add cream and reheat, do not boil.

Serve in heated individual bowls and garnish with croutons (see p. 63).

Serves 6.

§ CAULIFLOWER SOUP

This is a delicate creamy soup. You cannot make a meal from it, but it is delicious with sandwiches for lunch or served as a first course.

1 medium cauliflower, washed
1 stalk celery, washed and cut
  into 1-inch pieces
1 thick slice of lemon
2 tbs. butter
1 medium onion, peeled and
  diced
2 tbs. flour

1 cup of the water in which the
  cauliflower was cooked
3 cups of basic stock or chicken
  stock from which all fat has
  been removed
2 tsps. salt
¼ tsp. pepper
1 cup light cream

Cook the cauliflower, celery pieces and slice of lemon in boiling water. When tender, drain and reserve the celery pieces and 1 cup of the water. Discard the lemon.

Break the cauliflower into florets and reserve ½ cup of the tiniest for garnish.

Melt the butter in a large pot, and when foaming, add the onion. Stir and cook until transparent. Add the flour, cook and stir until well blended. Slowly add the cup of cauliflower water, stirring constantly, until well blended. Add the stock, salt and pepper. Put this mixture through a food mill or in a blender and blend until smooth.

Return the soup to the pot and simmer for 10 to 15 minutes. Add the light cream. Stir and bring to a boil. Just before serving, add the florets. Serve from a heated tureen or in individual bowls. Serves 6.

1498144

§ CREAM OF CARROT SOUP

This is a very thick soup. Its flavor is subtle, and its color is a soft lobster pink. I think you will enjoy serving it before a grilled fish entrée or an omelet supper.

2½ tbs. butter
2 cups carrots, scrubbed and
  diced
2 medium onions, peeled and
  diced
2 tbs. flour

1½ cups basic stock or beef
  stock from which all fat
  has been removed
1½ tsps. salt
⅛ tsp. pepper
2 whole cloves
1½ cups milk
Watercress leaves

Melt the butter in a heavy pot, and when foaming, add carrots and onions. Stir and cook until the onions are transparent. Add flour. Add stock slowly, and stir until the mixture is well blended. Add salt, pepper and cloves. Cover and simmer slowly for 30 minutes.

Remove the cloves and put the mixture through a food mill or blend in a blender until smooth. Return the soup to the pot and add the milk. Stir until it comes to a boil. Do not boil.

Serve in warmed individual soup bowls and float one or two watercress leaves on the top.

Serves 6.

§ CREAM OF CELERY SOUP

Celery happens to be one of my favorite vegetables, so I restrain myself in praising this soup as much as I would like, since I cannot be objective. It freezes perfectly; thaw it over a low heat or in a double boiler.

½ cup butter
1 large onion, peeled and coarsely chopped
3 cups celery, washed and cut in 1-inch pieces
2 medium potatoes, peeled and cubed

1 cup basic stock or chicken stock from which all fat has been removed
1 bay leaf
2 tsps. salt
½ tsp. pepper
2 cups milk
2 tbs. celery leaves, finely chopped

Melt the butter in a large, heavy pot; when foaming, add onion. Stir and cook until golden. Add celery, potatoes, stock, bay leaf, salt and pepper. Bring to a boil. Adjust heat to a simmer, cover with a loose-fitting lid and simmer for 30 minutes, or until potatoes are soft.

Remove bay leaf and put mixture through a food mill or blend in a blender until smooth. Return to the pot and add the milk. Heat.

Serve in warm soup bowls and garnish with the chopped celery leaves.

Serves 6.

§ CELERY AND EGG SOUP

Another delicious celery soup!

During my preschool years I was raised on a remote cattle ranch in Arizona by kind, elderly grandparents from New England. From them I first heard and experienced the strict application of such adages as "waste not, want not" and "a penny saved is a penny earned." Therefore, I cannot bring myself to discard the strained celery, carrot and onion left over from this recipe. I put them into a container, freeze them and add them to the pot when I prepare basic stock.

2 quarts basic stock or chicken stock from which all fat has been removed
1 medium onion, peeled and chopped
1 carrot, scrubbed and diced
12 stalks celery, including leaves, washed and cut into 1-inch pieces

1 tsp. salt
3 egg yolks
1 tbs. lemon juice
6 or 8 lemon slices, cut paper thin
2 tbs. celery leaves, finely chopped

Put the stock, onion, carrot, celery and salt into a large heavy pot. Bring to a boil, place a loose-fitting lid on top, adjust heat to a simmer, and simmer for 1 hour. Strain. Set this broth aside until final preparation time. In fact, it can be made a week or two in advance and frozen.

When ready to serve, bring the broth to a boil. Beat the egg yolks lightly with the lemon juice. Pour the hot broth into the egg yolks bit by bit, stirring constantly. When it is all well mixed, pour back into the pot and place over a low fire. Stirring constantly, cook for 3 or 4 minutes. Do not boil.

To serve: Pour into heated soup bowls and float a lemon slice on top and garnish with a sprinkling of the celery leaves.

Serves 6 to 8.

§ CREAM OF PEA AND MUSHROOM SOUP

This soup is such a vivid green that I feel it should be served by anyone of Irish ancestry on St. Patrick's Day. But don't look for an Irish ancestor, or wait until St. Patrick's Day, to try it. It is nourishing and delicious and can be frozen.

½ lb. mushrooms
2 tbs. butter
Lemon juice
2 tbs. flour
1½ cups basic stock or chicken stock from which all fat has been removed
½ tsp. chervil
2 tsps. salt
1 pinch cayenne pepper

2½ cups fresh peas, or frozen peas
1 quart milk
1 small onion, peeled and finely sliced
2 whole cloves
1 small bay leaf, crushed
1 clove garlic, peeled and finely diced
1 tbs. parsley, finely chopped

Clean the mushrooms and chop them coarsely. In a heavy pot melt the butter until foaming, add a few drops of lemon juice, add the mushrooms and cook over a high heat for 1 minute, stirring constantly. Lower heat and stir in flour, mix until smooth. Add 1 cup of stock slowly, stirring until well blended. Add chervil, salt and pepper. Bring to a boil. Adjust heat to a simmer, place a loose-fitting lid on top and simmer for 25 minutes. Give the pot an occasional stir.

Cook the peas in the remaining half cup of stock until tender. (If frozen peas are used follow the same procedure.) Put them, together with the water in which they were cooked, through a food mill, or blend in a blender until smooth. Add the pea purée to the mushroom mixture. Set aside.

Scald the milk with the onion, cloves, bay leaf, garlic and parsley in a sauce pan. Strain. Add the strained milk to the pea and mushroom mixture. Stir thoroughly and heat.

Serve from a heated tureen or heated individual soup bowls.

Serves 6.

§ CREAM OF CHICKEN AND VEGETABLE SOUP

This is too filling to serve as a first course. Plan it as a main dish with fresh dark bread and a crisp green salad with cheese. It freezes perfectly.

2 quarts basic stock or chicken stock from which all fat has been removed
1 tbs. potato flour
¼ cup cold water
1 tbs. butter
1 cup carrots, peeled and finely diced
1 cup celery, washed and finely diced

1 cup onions, peeled and finely diced
3 to 4 cups cooked chicken meat, diced
1 cup peas, fresh or frozen
2 tsps. salt
1 tsp. pepper
2 egg yolks, lightly beaten
½ cup heavy cream

Bring the stock to a boil. Mix potato flour with the water, and stirring, slowly pour into the stock and simmer.

Melt the butter in a pan, add carrots, celery and onions. Sauté for 5 to 10 minutes or until onions are transparent, not brown. Add to stock. Add chicken meat and simmer for 15 minutes. Add peas, salt and pepper and simmer 5 minutes.

Mix together the egg yolks and cream. Bit by bit add a small amount of the hot soup to the eggs and cream, stirring constantly. When a cup of the hot soup is blended with the egg mixture, pour it slowly into the soup, stirring continuously. Heat, but do not boil.

Serve from a heated tureen or in heated individual soup plates. Serves 6 to 8.

§ CHICKEN CURRY SOUP

A country cousin of an elegant Senegalese Soup, Chicken Curry Soup is similar, but quite a bit more filling, and the fried chicken pieces add a pleasant surprise. Should you want to make this a one-dish meal, put a cup of cooked rice into each soup plate and ladle the hot soup over it.

This recipe may be prepared a day or two in advance up to the point of frying the chicken pieces.

3 cups basic stock or chicken stock from which all fat has been removed
3 cups cold water
2 2½-lb. chickens split in half
1 large onion, peeled and quartered
1 large carrot, scrubbed and quartered

6 tbs. flour
4 tsps. curry powder
1 tsp. salt
1 pinch cayenne pepper
4 tsps. cornstarch
Seasoned flour
3 tbs. butter
¾ cup heavy cream
1 tbs. chives, finely chopped

Put the stock and water into a large heavy pot. Add the split chickens, onion and carrot and cover with a loose-fitting lid. Bring slowly to a boil. Adjust the heat to a simmer, and simmer for 25 to 30 minutes. Remove the pot from the heat, and cool the chickens in the broth.

When cool, remove the chickens and reserve the broth. Remove and discard the skin and bones of the chickens. Carve the meat into 2-inch pieces. Set aside.

Remove the fat from the broth. Strain the broth and return it to the pot.

Mix the flour, curry powder, salt, pepper and cornstarch to a smooth paste with cold water. Pour slowly into the broth, and bring the mixture to a boil, stirring continuously. When well blended, cover and simmer for 10 or 15 minutes.

When ready to serve, proceed as follows: Dredge the chicken pieces in the seasoned flour. Melt the butter in a frying pan, and when foaming, add the chicken pieces. Brown rapidly until crisp and golden. Add them to the soup, and simmer for 5 minutes. Add the cream, and heat; do not boil.

Serve in heated deep soup plates, and garnish with chives.
Serves 6.

§ *TOMATO AND DILL SOUP*

An ideal soup for the summer when you can get large, sun-ripened tomatoes. It may be served hot or chilled.

2 tbs. vegetable oil
1 medium onion, peeled and
 finely chopped
½ tsp. garlic, finely chopped
2 tsps. salt
½ tsp. pepper
6 large fresh tomatoes

1 tbs. tomato paste
3 tbs. flour
3 cups basic stock or chicken
 stock from which all fat
 has been removed
½ cup heavy cream
2 tbs. fresh dill, finely chopped

Heat the oil in a deep pot, add onion and garlic. Cook, stirring continuously, over medium heat for 2 minutes. Add salt and pepper and 2 of the tomatoes, which have been coarsely sliced, including the skin. Turn the heat up high and stir, cooking briskly for 3 minutes. Remove from the fire and add tomato paste, flour and stock. Return the pot to the fire, and bring to a boil, stirring continuously. Adjust heat to a simmer and simmer for 10 minutes.

Coarsely chop 2 more of the tomatoes including the skin and add to the mixture. Immediately put the soup through a fine strainer so that all seeds are removed.

Return the soup to a pot, add the cream, dill and the last 2 tomatoes, which have been peeled, seeded and cut in fine, thin shreds. Heat, do not boil.

To serve hot: Pour at once into a large heated tureen or heated individual bowls.

To serve cold: Chill for 4 hours or overnight in the refrigerator. Stir and pour into chilled individual bowls.

Serves 6.

§ SORREL SOUP

The special tartness of sorrel, which is also known as sourgrass, makes this an especially delectable early-summer soup. When the sorrel is in season, pick the freshest, tenderest leaves; bruised or wilted leaves do not make a good soup.

1 lb. fresh sorrel leaves
3 tbs. butter
1 medium onion, peeled and
 finely chopped
2 egg yolks
1 cup light cream

4 cups basic stock or chicken
 stock from which all fat
 has been removed
1 tsp. salt
¼ tsp. pepper
Croutons

Wash sorrel leaves thoroughly and dry them. Cut into fine shreds and set aside.

In a heavy, small pot, melt butter, and when foaming, add onion and cook until transparent. Add sorrel leaves, stir, turn off heat and cover with a lid.

Beat egg yolks lightly. Add cream and mix until blended.

In a large heavy pot heat the stock until it comes to a boil. Lower the heat and slowly, stirring briskly, add the cream and egg yolk mixture. Add the sorrel and onion, salt and pepper. Stir and heat; do not boil.

Serve in a heated tureen or heated individual bowls. Garnish with croutons (see p. 63).

Serves 6.

§ MINESTRONE

A *friend of mine, well known for her culinary skills, said she found minestrone an ideal dish for the end of the Christmas holiday season, as it is simple and delicious. Serve it with a crisp green salad, French bread and a fruit compote. It freezes perfectly.*

¼ cup kidney beans
¼ cup small lima beans
¼ cup olive oil
2 cups spinach leaves, washed and chopped
1 cup celery, washed and diced
3 cups cabbage, shredded
2 cups scrubbed carrots, diced
1 medium onion, peeled and coarsely chopped
2 tbs. parsley, finely chopped

1 clove garlic, peeled and finely chopped
2 quarts basic, brown or beef stock from which all fat has been removed
2 cups canned tomatoes
½ cup rice
½ tsp. thyme
¼ tsp. rosemary
1 pinch sage
2½ tsps. salt
1 tsp. pepper
½ cup elbow macaroni

Combine the kidney and lima beans in a bowl; cover with cold water and soak overnight. Drain.

Heat the olive oil in a large pot and add the spinach, celery, cabbage, carrots, onion, parsley and garlic. Sauté for 5 minutes

over a high heat, stirring all the while. Add the beans, stock, tomatoes, rice, thyme, rosemary, sage, salt and pepper. Stir. Bring to a
boil, cover with a lid and adjust the heat to a simmer. Simmer for
1½ hours, stirring occasionally. Add macaroni and continue to
cook another half-hour, or until the beans are tender.

Serve in a heated serving dish.

This recipe makes 3 quarts.

Variation: Add ½ cup of any in-season vegetable, diced: string
beans, wax beans, peas, turnips, etc.

§ LENTIL SOUP

*A fine soup for any time of the year. It freezes well, and there
are so many variations possible in serving it, that with a quart or
two on hand a nutritious and tasteful dinner can be rapidly prepared.*

1 lb. dried lentils
7 cups cold water
1 ham bone
2 stalks celery, washed and
    coarsely chopped
2 carrots, washed and quartered
2 medium onions, peeled and
    coarsely chopped
1 small clove garlic, peeled and
    chopped

4 tsps. salt
1 tsp. pepper
3 sprigs parsley
1 small bay leaf
2 tbs. lemon juice
2 cups basic stock or ham stock
    from which all fat has been
    removed

Wash lentils and put them into a large, heavy pot. Add all the
other ingredients except the stock. Stir. Put a loose-fitting lid on
top of the pot, bring to a boil, adjust heat to a simmer and simmer
for 1 hour. Remove the ham bone.

Put the soup through a food mill, and don't be lazy in extract-
ing all the goodness from the lentils; you should have to discard no
more than the tough husks.

Return the purée to the pot, and add the stock. Stir and bring
to a boil.

This recipe makes 2 quarts.

To serve: Select one of the following variations:

a) Add neatly diced cubes of cooked ham.

b) Add frankfurters cut in ½-inch pieces and simmered 10 minutes in the soup.

c) Serve with croutons (see p. 63).

d) Float a thin lemon slice on each bowl.

e) To each quart of soup add 1 cup of light cream, stir, heat and serve.

§ WHITE BEAN SOUP

Not for the calorie counter but for anyone who enjoys a hearty, rich soup. It can be made with the Great Northern white bean or the small navy bean. It freezes perfectly.

4 cups white beans, cooked and drained	½ tsp. pepper
1 cup basic, chicken or beef stock from which all fat has been removed	1 cup tomato sauce (canned)
	1 cup cooked rice
	1 cup watercress leaves, stemmed and washed
1 tsp. lemon juice	Butter
1 tsp. salt	Heavy cream

Put the beans and stock together through a food mill or into a blender and blend until smooth. Pour the mixture into a large, heavy pot, and add the lemon juice, salt, pepper, tomato sauce and rice. Stir and bring to a boil. Add the watercress leaves, stir and cook until they are wilted, approximately 2 to 3 minutes.

Serve piping hot in heated individual soup bowls, and top each serving with a small nugget of butter and a teaspoon of heavy cream.

Serves 6.

Variation: Sorrel can be added instead of watercress and is prepared as follows:

Wash and finely shred enough fresh sorrel leaves to make ½ cup. Add them to the hot soup and simmer for 10 to 15 minutes.

§ PEASANT SOUP

Here is an outstandingly delicious and hearty soup. With great patience and time it could be prepared in a regular pot, but I would not care to tackle it without using a pressure cooker.

I have divided the recipe into six parts; each is simple and can be completed as your time allows. The final result is well worth the effort.

Peasant soup freezes excellently, and the large quantity provided by following the recipe should be sufficient for two or three suppers.

This recipe was originated by Mrs. Charles Roome.

PART 1

3½ lbs. lamb shanks
6 cups basic or brown stock
    from which all fat has
    been removed
1 large onion, peeled and
    coarsely chopped

1 stalk celery, including
    leaves, cut into 3-inch
    pieces
1 bay leaf

Have your butcher crack the lamb shanks into 4-inch pieces. Put them in a 4-quart pressure cooker; add stock, onion, celery, and bay leaf. Cook at 10 pounds of pressure for 1 hour. Reduce pressure immediately. Strain broth into a bowl, cool and refrigerate. Set the lamb in a dish to cool and refrigerate.

PART 2

¼ cup each of dried kidney
    beans, black-eyed peas,
    pinto beans, pea beans,
    small lima beans, black tur-
    tle beans and whole green
    peas

½ tsp. thyme
1 clove garlic, peeled and finely
    chopped
2 tsps. salt

Soak the beans and peas in cold water overnight. In the morning drain off the water, and put beans and peas in a 4-quart pressure cooker with the thyme, garlic and salt. Add cold water to within 2 inches from the top of the cooker.

Set the pressure at 15 pounds, and when pressure is reached, cook for 5 minutes. Allow the pressure to go down of its own accord, then pour into a large 8- to 10-quart soup pot.

PART 3

½ cup barley
½ tsp. thyme
¼ cup each of dried green split peas, yellow peas, lentils and brown rice

1 clove garlic, peeled and finely chopped
2 tsps. salt

Put all ingredients into a 4-quart pressure cooker, and cover with cold water to within 2 inches from the top. Set pressure gauge at 15 pounds, and when pressure is reached, cook for 5 minutes. Allow the pressure to go down of its own accord, then pour into the soup pot with the beans.

PART 4

1 cup carrots, scrubbed and diced
1 cup celery stalks, washed and diced
1 cup onions, peeled and diced

1 cup potatoes, peeled and diced
½ tsp. thyme
1 clove garlic, peeled and finely chopped
2 tsps. salt

Put all the ingredients into a saucepan, and cover with boiling water. Cover with a lid, and simmer for 20 minutes. Pour all of this into the soup pot.

PART 5

1 lb. pork sausages

Fry the sausages until brown. Discard the fat. Cut them into 1-inch pieces, and add them to the soup pot.

PART 6

Cold stock
Cold lamb
6 tbs. parsley, finely chopped
4 tbs. celery leaves, finely chopped

1 clove garlic, peeled and finely chopped
1½ tsps. pepper
¼ lb. sweet butter

Remove all the fat from the stock in which the lamb was cooked, and add it to the soup pot.

Remove all the fat and bones from the lamb, and cut the meat into ½-inch cubes. Add to the soup pot.

To the soup pot add the parsley, celery leaves, garlic, pepper and butter. Bring to a boil, adjust heat to a simmer, and simmer for 30 minutes.

The soup is now ready to serve, and a heated tureen is an ideal serving dish. The soup can be refrigerated, reheated and served the following day, or it can be poured into containers and frozen for future use.

This recipe makes 6 to 7 quarts.

§ BRAIN SOUP VIENNESE

The great chef Escoffier wrote that "calf's brains form the most wholesome rebuilding diet for all those who are weakened by excessive head-work. . . ." I do not believe that present-day nutritionists would agree, but I do believe that they would agree this is a good soup. It is elegant to the eye, and if your family or friends are squeamish about eating brains, do not tell them what they're eating, just serve the soup.

1 pair calf's brains, cleaned
8 tbs. butter
2 tbs. flour
4 cups basic or brown stock from which all fat has been removed

6 tbs. parsley, finely chopped
1 tsp. salt
½ tsp. pepper

Clean the brains by covering them with cold water and soaking for 20 or 30 minutes. Remove and wash under cold running water.

Cover again with cold water to which a dash of salt or vinegar has been added and leave for 15 minutes. Remove and wash under cold running water. Carefully remove all the membrane and veins.

In a small pot melt 4 tablespoons of the butter, and when foaming, add the brains. Sauté over a medium heat for 20 minutes. Remove the brains and set aside on paper towels, or brown paper, to absorb the excess butter.

In a heavy pot melt the other 4 tablespoons of butter and add flour. Cook, stirring constantly, until flour and butter are a deep, rich brown. Remove from heat and stir in 1 cup of stock. Return to heat and stir until flour and stock are smoothly blended. Add the balance of the stock, 4 tablespoons of parsley, salt and pepper. Cover with a loose-fitting lid and simmer for 15 minutes.

Cut the sautéed brains into tiny pieces, about the size of a navy bean, add to the soup and simmer for 5 minutes.

Serve in heated individual soup bowls, and garnish with the balance of the chopped parsley.

Serves 6.

§ EGG AND MEAT SOUP

A delightful use for leftover roast, boiled beef or chicken. An excellent soup for a quick, nourishing lunch.

6 cups basic or beef stock
    from which all fat has
    been removed
2 tsps. soy sauce
1 tsp. salt
¼ tsp. pepper

2 eggs
2 tbs. lemon juice
1½ cups cooked beef or chicken
    meat, finely diced
Parsley, finely chopped

Bring the stock to a boil in a heavy pot, add soy sauce, salt and pepper. Beat eggs lightly. Stirring the stock rapidly, pour the eggs slowly into the pot. Add lemon juice and meat. Simmer for 2 or 3 minutes.

Serve at once in heated individual bowls, and garnish with parsley.

Serves 6.

§ HUNGARIAN GOULASH SOUP

In the pre-World War II days of Vienna, after the balls, and particularly during the festivities of Mardi Gras, it was customary for the revelers to stop at a restaurant before going home and consume a large bowl of this soup. Served scalding hot, it was supposed to cure any ill effect one might have from drinking too much wine or champagne. I regret I cannot say whether it is effective in this regard or not, but I can say that it is an excellent soup in any season. It freezes perfectly.

1 lb. beef, shin or chuck
¼ lb. bacon, cut into 1-inch pieces
4 medium onions, peeled and coarsely chopped
2 tsps. paprika
½ tsp. caraway seeds
1 pinch marjoram
1 clove garlic, peeled and finely chopped
6 cups basic stock or beef stock from which all fat has been removed

2 cups canned tomatoes
1 tsp. salt
¼ cup red wine
1 tbs. tomato paste
½ tsp. sugar
¼ tsp. pepper
3 medium potatoes, peeled and cubed into ½-inch pieces
¼ cup flour
¾ cup water
4 beef frankfurters, cooked
Lemon juice

Cube the beef into ½-inch pieces, discarding excess fat and tough cartilage.

Fry the bacon in a large heavy pot until it is clear. Add the onions and cook until golden, stirring constantly. Add the paprika, caraway seeds, marjoram and garlic, and stir and cook for one or two minutes.

Add the stock, tomatoes, salt, wine, tomato paste, sugar and pepper. Bring to a boil. Stir. Place a loose-fitting lid on the pot, adjust heat to a simmer and simmer for 25 minutes.

Add the potatoes and simmer 30 minutes or until tender.

Mix the flour and water until they make a smooth paste, and pour it slowly into the soup stirring all the while. Simmer until the soup thickens.

Slice the frankfurters into ¼-inch pieces, and add them to the soup together with a few drops of lemon juice. Stir and simmer for 5 minutes.

Serve piping hot in large heated soup plates.

Serves 6 to 8.

§ SMOKED BACON AND LEEK SOUP

Buy the smokiest-flavored bacon your butcher has on hand for this soup. I find that smoked slab bacon is best.

¼ lb. smoked bacon, sliced and cut into ½-inch pieces

6 cups basic stock or ham stock from which all fat has been removed

4 medium leeks, including the fresh green leaves, split in half, washed and cut in thin slices

2 medium potatoes, peeled and cubed into ¼-inch pieces

¼ lb. smoked cooked ham, cut in thin strips (the size of a kitchen match)

1½ tsps. salt

½ tsp. pepper

Fry the bacon pieces over a low fire until they are transparent, not crisp. Discard the fat and drain the pieces on a paper towel.

Bring the stock to a boil in a large pot, and add the leeks, potatoes and bacon. Bring the soup to a boil and place a loose-fitting lid on top. Turn the heat down to a simmer, and simmer for 30 minutes or until potatoes are tender. Add the ham strips, salt and pepper and simmer for 10 minutes.

Pour into a heated tureen and serve at once.

Serves 6.

Note: If ham stock is used, taste before adding salt.

§ GREEN BEAN AND BACON SOUP

Here is a real country soup. Serve it as the main dish with hot cornbread. It is easy to prepare and freezes excellently.

½ lb. smoked bacon
2 cups string beans, washed and
    cut into 1-inch pieces
1 cup onions, chopped fine
6 cups basic stock or beef stock
    from which all fat has been
    removed

2 tsps. tomato paste
2 tsps. salt
½ tsp. pepper
⅔ cup rice

Cut the bacon in ½-inch pieces, and fry over a low flame until transparent. Do not brown. Discard all the bacon fat except 2 teaspoons. Drain the bacon pieces on a paper towel.

Add the string beans and onions to the bacon fat, and sauté for 5 to 10 minutes, or until onions are transparent, not brown.

Bring the stock to a boil, add bacon, onion, beans, tomato paste, salt, pepper and rice. Cover with a loose-fitting lid, adjust flame to a simmer and simmer for 25 to 30 minutes, or until rice and beans are tender.

Serve in a heated tureen or in large, heated soup plates.
Serves 6.

Variation: Ham may be substituted for the bacon; dice into small pieces, and sauté the onions and beans in butter.

§ SUMMER SOUP

A hearty, nutritious soup, equally good in winter, and definitely a one-dish meal. I think it is the sweetness of the green peppers that gives it such a light, cool flavor.

2 large green peppers, washed
2 slices bacon, cut into ½-inch
    pieces
1 large onion, peeled and finely
    chopped
1 quart basic stock or beef
    stock from which all fat
    has been removed
½ cup red wine

1 clove garlic, peeled and finely
    chopped
2 tsps. salt
½ tsp. pepper
½ tsp. thyme
½ tsp. sugar
1 lb. lean ground chuck or bot-
    tom round of beef
2 cups canned tomatoes

Remove the core, seeds and white membranes from the green peppers. Dice into small pieces.

Fry the bacon pieces until most of their fat is rendered, but do not brown. Add diced peppers and onions; cook and stir until the onions are transparent. Pour this mixture into a large, heavy pot. Add stock, wine, garlic, salt, pepper, thyme, sugar, beef and tomatoes. If the tomatoes are whole, dice them into small pieces.

When adding the beef, break it up so that it does not form large lumps.

Cover with a loose-fitting lid. Bring to a boil, adjust heat to a simmer and simmer for 1 hour.

Serve in the pot, or pour into a heated tureen.

Serves 6.

§ WINTERBORSCHT (BEETS AND BEEF SOUP)

A warming, nourishing soup, particularly good in winter, and pleasing to the eye.

3 cups water
3 cups basic stock or brown stock from which all fat has been removed
3 lbs. short ribs of beef
2 medium onions, peeled and sliced thin
3 stalks celery, washed and cut into 2-inch pieces
4 large beets, peeled and sliced
4 carrots, scrubbed and sliced
1 tbs. salt

1 bay leaf
1 cup beets, peeled and cut into thin strips
1 6-oz. can tomato paste
2 tbs. vinegar
1 tbs. sugar
1 tbs. salt
6 Idaho baking potatoes
1 head cabbage, cut into 8 wedges
2 tbs. dill, finely chopped
1 cup sour cream

Put water, stock, ribs of beef, onions, celery, beets, carrots, salt and bay leaf into a large pot. Cover with a loose-fitting lid and simmer for 2 hours.

Add the strips of beets, tomato paste, vinegar, sugar and salt. Bring to a simmer, and simmer for 20 minutes.

Remove from fire, cool and refrigerate. When cold, discard all the fat congealed on the surface. Remove and discard the beef bones. Cut the meat into neat serving pieces. At this point the soup can be frozen or set aside. 1 hour before serving proceed as follows:

Steam or boil the potatoes in a separate pot for 40 to 50 minutes, or until tender. Peel the potatoes and keep them warm.

While the potatoes are cooking, bring the soup to a boil. Add the cabbage wedges and cook 20 to 25 minutes.

To serve: Heat six large, deep soup plates. Into each, spoon a wedge of cabbage, a few pieces of meat and a generous ladleful of the soup. Roll the potatoes in the chopped dill, and place one into each plate. Put a heaping tablespoon of sour cream into the center of each plate. Serve immediately.

Serves 6.

§ MUSHROOM SOUP JOSEPHINE

This is a low-calorie soup with real flavor. It is very simple to prepare and can be frozen.

1 lb. fresh or frozen mush-
    rooms
4 tbs. butter
½ tsp. lemon juice
4 cups basic stock or brown
    stock from which all fat
    has been removed

1 tsp. salt
4 tsps. soy sauce
1½ tbs. potato flour
3 tbs. cold water
2 tbs. sherry

Clean the mushrooms. Set aside 4 mushroom caps. Coarsely chop the balance of the mushrooms, including the stems.

Melt the butter in a large pot, and when foaming, add mushrooms and ¼ teaspoon of the lemon juice. Cook over a high heat for 3 or 4 minutes, stirring constantly. Add stock, salt and soy sauce. Cover with a loose-fitting lid, and simmer for 5 minutes.

Put the mixture into a blender, and blend until smooth, or mash through a food mill. Pour it back into the pot, and bring to a simmer.

Mix the potato flour with the cold water, and stir into the soup. Stir and cook until it is thickened.

Finely dice the raw mushroom caps and add to the soup. Simmer for 5 minutes without a cover on the pot. Add the balance of the lemon juice. Just before serving, add the sherry.

To serve: Pour into heated individual soup bowls.
Serves 6.

§ ONION SOUP

The excellence of this soup depends upon your basic or brown stock, which should be strong and full-bodied. Don't be in a rush to boil it up fast to tenderize the onions; rather let it simmer slowly so that the stock and onions meld their flavors.

2 tbs. butter	8 cups hot basic stock or brown
2 tbs. vegetable oil	stock from which all fat
4 cups onions, peeled and sliced	has been removed
into thin rings	¼ cup brandy
½ tsp. sugar	6 or 8 thick slices French
2 tbs. flour	bread, toasted
1 tsp. salt	1 cup grated Swiss cheese
¼ tsp. pepper	

Melt the butter and oil in a large, heavy pot and add onion rings. Separate the rings as they are added. Keep the heat low, and cook slowly until the onions are transparent. Add the sugar and cook and stir until the onions are an even golden brown. Sprinkle on the flour and mix well. Add salt and pepper.

Remove from heat and slowly add stock, stirring continuously. When well blended, return to the fire and bring to a boil. Adjust heat to a simmer, cover with a loose-fitting lid and simmer for 35 to 45 minutes. Add brandy.

To serve: Ladle the soup into heated individual deep soup bowls, place a piece of toasted French bread on each and heap a generous tablespoon of cheese on top of each. Place under the broiler until the cheese has melted and is lightly browned. Serve immediately.
Serves 6 to 8.

§ QUICK VEGETABLE SOUP

With your stock on hand, this soup is quick, easy, delicious and nutritious, and its variations are limited only by your imagination. Any fresh vegetables in season are a welcome addition.

6 cups basic stock or beef stock from which all fat has been removed

2 cups potatoes, peeled and diced

2 cups carrots, peeled and diced

1 medium onion, peeled and thinly sliced

4 stalks celery, washed and diced

1 small clove garlic, finely chopped

2 leeks, washed and only the white part thinly sliced

1 cup canned tomatoes

1 cup noodles

1 cup fresh spinach, washed and chopped, or frozen chopped spinach

2 tsps. salt

1 tsp. pepper

3 tbs. parsley, finely chopped

Put the stock into a large pot and bring to a boil. Add all the ingredients but the parsley, and bring the pot back to a boil. Adjust heat to a simmer, cover with a loose-fitting lid and simmer for 20 to 30 minutes, or until vegetables are tender.

Serve in heated individual soup plates, or from a heated tureen. Garnish with the parsley.

Serves 6 to 8.

Variation: Add 2 cups of cubed cooked beef.

§ SOUP ALEXANDER

This recipe was given to me by a friend, Alexander, after whom I've named it. He brought it home from one of his visits to Greece. It demands a heady, pungent stock; any scraps and bones from a lamb roast can be added to the stock.

Lamb stock is not included in the chapter on stocks because, in my opinion, its strong and distinctive flavor limits its use. How-

ever, this soup is so delicious it is worth making. A greater quantity of stock may be made and frozen for future use.

LAMB STOCK

2 to 3 lbs. lamb shanks	1 stalk celery, washed and coarsely sliced
1 carrot, scrubbed and quartered	1 tsp. thyme
1 medium onion, peeled and quartered	3 tsps. salt
	8 peppercorns
1 clove garlic, peeled and halved	¼ cup dry white wine, or lemon juice
1 bay leaf	2½ quarts cold water

Place all the ingredients in a large pot, bring to a boil, cover with a loose-fitting lid, adjust the heat to a simmer and simmer 3 to 4 hours. During the last hour of cooking, remove the lid, turn the heat up high and reduce the stock to 8 cups.

Strain the stock into a bowl and cool. Remove the fat, and prepare the soup as follows:

MAKING THE SOUP

8 cups lamb stock from which all fat has been removed	1 tbs. lemon juice
½ cup rice	2 egg yolks
	Mint leaves, finely shredded

Put the stock into a large pot, and when boiling, add the rice. Cover, adjust heat to a simmer and cook until the rice is tender. When tender, add the lemon juice and stir.

Beat the egg yolks slightly in a small bowl. Remove the soup from the heat, and with a long-handled wooden spoon or fork stir the soup rapidly, and while stirring, slowly pour the yolks into it in a thin stream. Serve at once in heated individual bowls, and garnish with the mint.

Serves 6.

Variation: Instead of garnishing with the mint, float a paper-thin slice of lemon in each bowl.

§ CHEESE SOUP

Delicious, economical and easy to prepare. Use a good strong Vermont natural cheddar, sometimes called "store cheese." For a summer luncheon serve this soup with a fruit salad and French bread. In winter it is good anytime and perfect after a day on the ski slopes.

4 tbs. butter	3 cups milk
2 cups onions, peeled and finely chopped	3 tsps. salt
4 tbs. flour	1 tsp. pepper
3 cups basic stock or beef stock from which all fat has been removed	2½ cups cheddar cheese, grated and firmly packed into the measuring cups

Melt the butter in a large pot, and when foaming, add the onions. Stir and cook until transparent. Add flour and stir and cook over a low heat for 5 minutes. Do not brown.

Remove the pot from the heat, and add the stock bit by bit, stirring all the while. Return to the heat and bring to a boil. Simmer for 5 to 10 minutes, giving the pot an occasional stir. Add the milk, salt and pepper. Stir and bring to a boil. Add the cheese, stir and bring to a boil.

Serve piping hot in heated mugs or bowls.

Serves 6 to 8.

§ CRAB CHOWDER

2 tbs. butter	1 tsp. fresh dill, finely chopped
2 cups onions, finely chopped	1 tsp. salt
½ tsp. garlic, finely chopped	½ tsp. pepper
3 fillets of sole or haddock cut into ½-inch pieces	½ lb. crab flakes
1 cup mushrooms, finely chopped	2 cups fish stock
	2 cups heavy cream

Melt the butter in a deep pot, add onions and garlic and cook until soft. Add fillets, mushrooms, dill, salt and pepper. Cook, stirring constantly, 3 or 4 minutes. Add crab flakes. Slowly stir in the fish stock and cream. Bring to a simmer, and simmer for 2 or 3 minutes. Serve at once.

Serve from a large heated tureen or in heated individual bowls. Serves 6.

Variation: Crab chunks cut into small pieces may be substituted for the crab flakes.

§ SCALLOP CHOWDER

2 ozs. salt pork, finely diced
2 cups onions, chopped fine
3 cups potatoes, peeled and
　　diced in ½-inch pieces
6 cups fish stock
2 tomatoes, peeled, seeded and
　　finely chopped
2 tsps. salt
½ tsp. pepper
1 lb. scallops
4 saltine crackers, finely crumbled
1 cup heavy cream
Parsley, finely chopped

Fry the salt pork pieces in a large heavy pot until golden brown. Discard all but 1 tablespoon of the fat. Add onions and cook until transparent. Add potatoes and fish stock. Cook over a medium heat, with a loose-fitting lid on top, for 20 minutes, or until potatoes are tender. Add tomatoes, salt and pepper, and cook for 5 minutes. Add scallops, crackers and cream. Stir. Bring to a simmer, and simmer for 3 to 5 minutes.

Serve from a large heated tureen or in heated individual bowls. Garnish lightly with chopped parsley.

Serves 6 to 8.

Note: If sea scallops are used, cut them into small pieces.

§ HIGGINS' FISH CHOWDER

My sister has made her home on the coast of Maine for the past twenty-five years. This is the chowder served by the "downeasterners" on a Sunday night with crackers and a salad. The use of canned evaporated milk is "pure Maine"; it makes a richer soup, but the soup can be made with all fresh milk.

2 cups fish stock
2 cups water
2½ to 3 lbs. fillet of haddock
4 tbs. butter
1 large onion, peeled and
  finely chopped

1 quart of potatoes, peeled
  and diced into ½- to
  1-inch cubes
1⅓ cups fresh milk
⅔ cup canned evaporated milk
2 tsps. salt
½ tsp. pepper
Paprika

Combine the fish stock and water in a pot and bring to a boil. When boiling, drop the fish into it and cover. Adjust the heat to a simmer, and simmer until the fish flakes easily when tested with a fork. Remove the fish with a slotted spoon to a dish and break it into small pieces. Set aside. Reserve the stock.

Melt the butter in a large pot, and when hot, add onion and cook until transparent. Add potatoes and the reserved stock. Cover and cook until the potatoes are tender.

Meanwhile, combine the fresh and canned milk in a pan and scald.

When the potatoes are tender add to them the scalded milk, the fish pieces, salt and pepper. Heat, but do not boil.

To serve: Pour the chowder into a heated tureen, individual bowls, or serve it directly from the pot in which it was cooked. Garnish with a few dashes of paprika.

Serves 6.

§ *BILLI-BI*

A *splendid soup.*

2½ lbs. mussels
3 sprigs parsley
1 small bay leaf
1 stalk celery, finely diced
2 shallots, finely chopped
1 small onion, peeled and
  finely sliced
¼ tsp. thyme

6 peppercorns
2 tbs. butter
2 cups dry white wine
1½ cups heavy cream
1 cup fish stock
1 tsp. salt
¼ tsp. white pepper

Clean the mussels by scrubbing them with a strong brush under cold running water. Cut and scrape off the beards. Put the mussels into a large pot, cover with cold water and discard any mussels that float on the surface; also discard any mussels that are not closed. If a mussel is open or floats before it is cooked, it means that it is not fresh.

Put the parsley, bay leaf, celery, shallots, onion, thyme, peppercorns, butter and wine into a large pot. Add the cleaned mussels. Put a lid on top, bring to a boil and steam 5 to 10 minutes. All the shells should open; discard any mussels whose shell remains closed.

Remove the mussels from the pot with a slotted spoon and set aside. Line a strainer with 2 thicknesses of cheesecloth, and strain the liquid into a bowl.

Put the strained liquid into a pot, bring to a boil and add the cream, stock, salt and pepper. Stir and reheat. Do not boil.

Serve in small heated bowls. Cheese sticks are a perfect accompaniment to this soup.

Serves 4 to 6.

Note: The mussels should be removed from their shells, refrigerated and used to make a mussel bisque (see recipe this page).

Another use for the cold mussels is to mix them with a vinaigrette (see p. 178), add 2 tablespoons of finely chopped parsley and serve them as a first course.

A few mussel shells should be saved to garnish either the bisque or salad.

§ MUSSEL BISQUE

3 lbs. mussels	1 cup heavy cream
1 cup dry white wine	½ tsp. salt
1½ cups fish stock	1 pinch cayenne pepper
4 tbs. butter	1 pinch nutmeg
4 tbs. flour	1 tbs. brandy
2 cups milk	

Thoroughly scrub the mussels and remove the beards. Discard any mussels that are open, or that float.

Put the wine, fish stock and mussels into a large pot; cover with a tight-fitting lid and steam over a low heat until all the shells have opened, about 10 minutes. Remove the pot from the heat and cool.

When cool, remove the mussels from the shells and set aside. Discard any mussels that did not open.

Strain the broth into a bowl through a fine strainer lined with 2 layers of cheesecloth. Set aside.

Melt the butter in a large pot, and when foaming, add flour. Cook and stir 2 to 3 minutes. Do not brown. Remove from the heat, and slowly add 1 cup of the milk; stir and blend until smooth. Add the other cup of milk and the mussel broth, return to heat, stir and bring to a boil. Simmer and stir over a low heat, or over hot water, for 10 minutes.

Chop the mussels into small pieces and add to the bisque together with the cream, salt, pepper, nutmeg and brandy. Heat, but do not boil.

To serve: Pour into heated individual bowls, or serve from a heated tureen.

Serves 6.

Variation: If you have made the Billi-Bi Soup (see p. 59), use the mussels for this bisque. Follow the above recipe except use only ½ cup of dry white wine and 2½ cups of fish stock. Proceed with the recipe as given.

§ CREAMED SHRIMP SOUP

4 cups fish stock
¾ lb. shrimps, fresh or frozen
3 cups milk
1 small bay leaf
1 cup celery, finely diced
4 tbs. onion, peeled and finely
    chopped

4 tbs. parsley, finely chopped
1½ tsp. salt
½ tsp. pepper
4 tbs. butter
4 tbs. flour

Put the stock into a pot and bring to a boil. Add the fresh or frozen shrimps, cook 5 minutes, or until they have turned pink. Turn the heat off, and allow the shrimps to cool in the stock. Remove the shrimps from the stock with a slotted spoon. Strain and reserve the stock.

If fresh shrimps are used, peel and devein. Cut the shrimps into small pieces about the size of a raisin. Set aside.

Put the milk in a pan, add bay leaf, celery, onion, parsley, salt and pepper, and scald. Remove bay leaf.

Meanwhile, melt the butter in a large pot, and when foaming, add the flour, stir and cook over a low heat 3 or 4 minutes. Remove from heat. Add 3 cups of the strained fish stock in which the shrimps were cooked and the scalded milk together with the celery, onion and parsley. Stir and blend.

Return to heat, and stirring constantly, bring to a simmer, and simmer uncovered for 10 minutes. Add the shrimp pieces. Heat.

Serve from a heated tureen or in heated individual soup bowls. Serves 6.

§ TOMATO AND SHRIMP SOUP

This is a bit unusual because it combines fish stock and a meat stock, but I think you will like its flavor. It is perfect as the first course for a dinner party or a special luncheon.

6 large ripe tomatoes, quartered
2 cups canned tomatoes
3 large onions, peeled and
　　coarsely sliced
2 tbs. butter
1 clove garlic, peeled
1 bay leaf
2 medium carrots, scrubbed
　　and quartered
2 stalks celery, washed and
　　quartered

1 tsp. sugar
2 tsps. salt
¼ tsp. pepper
5 cups fish stock
1 lb. shrimps, fresh or frozen
3 cups basic stock or beef stock
　　from which all fat has been
　　removed
2 tbs. tomato paste
Dill or parsley, finely
　　chopped

Put the fresh tomatoes, canned tomatoes, onions, butter, garlic, bay leaf, carrots, celery, sugar, salt and pepper into a heavy pot.

Bring to a boil, cover with a loose-fitting lid and cook over a medium heat until the ingredients are soft, 25 to 35 minutes.

Meanwhile, put the fish stock into a pot, bring to a boil, add the shrimps and cook 5 minutes, or until they have turned pink. Turn the heat off and allow them to cool in the stock. Remove the shrimps with a slotted spoon and reserve the stock. If fresh shrimps are used, peel and devein. Set aside.

When the tomato mixture is soft, remove the bay leaf and mash the mixture through a food mill or a strainer. Do not put it in the blender, because the seeds and skins of the tomatoes are to be discarded.

Return the mashed tomato liquid to the pot. Cook and stir over a high heat, without a lid, until the liquid is reduced to a purée. The pot must be carefully watched and stirred during this step so that the purée does not burn. When reduced, there should be 3 cups of purée.

Add the basic stock or beef stock and tomato paste to the purée. Cut the shrimps into ½-inch pieces and add to the soup. Bring to a boil and serve.

Serve from a heated tureen or in heated individual bowls. Garnish with fresh dill or parsley.

Serves 6.

§ CROUTONS

Croutons are such a delightful garnish that I recommend preparing a whole loaf of bread at a time. Freeze what you don't immediately use in cup-size containers. To reheat, place them in a pan in a medium oven for 10 minutes. They will be as crisp and crunchy as if freshly made.

1 loaf white bread, thinly sliced   ½ lb. butter, melted

Cut the crusts from the bread. With a brush, brush each side of the bread slices with butter. Stack the slices evenly and cut them into small cubes. Place on a cookie sheet in a 350° F. oven. Shake and gently toss the bread cubes from time to time until they are all a deep golden brown.

Yield: 4 cups.

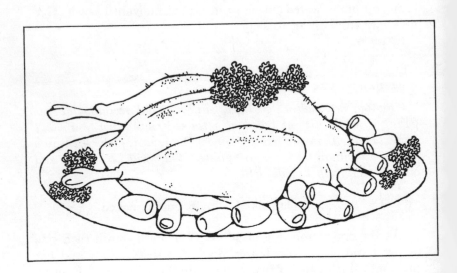

3 Poultry

POULTRY NOTES

THE MEAT OF CHICKEN is tender and succulent, but it loses both these qualities if it is cooked too long. Besides watching the cooking time given in the recipe, test whether the chicken is done from time to time by using one of the following methods:

a) A whole chicken is done when the leg can be moved easily to and fro.

b) A whole chicken is done if the juices run pale pink or clear when a fork is stuck into the upper joint of the second joint.

c) Chicken pieces are done if a fork easily pierces the thickest piece.

Veal stock may be substituted for chicken stock. Also canned chicken broth may be substituted for your own chicken stock, but the dish will not be as flavorful.

All dishes use freshly ground pepper. It is preferable to use freshly ground white peppercorns in chicken dishes with a white sauce.

If your family does not like the skin of chicken, it is easily removed from a boiled or steamed chicken a moment before serving.

A double boiler is a marvelous utensil to use in reheating frozen chicken or chicken in a sauce. Put it over a low flame, cover and let it reheat gently, steaming in its own juices.

Taste before you serve, and correct the seasoning to *your* taste.

§ BOILED CHICKEN DINNER

Instead of using the traditional old large fowl for this recipe, I prefer to use two young chickens. They cook more rapidly, and the vegetables can go into the pot as soon as the chickens are simmering.

2 2½- to 3-lb. chickens
½ lemon
4 cups cold basic stock or chicken stock from which all fat has been removed
1 bay leaf
4 sprigs parsley
3 sprigs celery leaves
1 large onion, peeled
2 tsps. salt
½ tsp. pepper

12 new white potatoes, scrubbed, or 8 medium potatoes, peeled and cut in half
6 large leeks, including the fresh green leaves, washed and cut in half
12 medium carrots, scrubbed and cut in half
1 lb. peas, fresh or frozen
2 tbs. parsley, finely chopped

Rub chickens inside and out with lemon, truss and place into a large pot. Add stock. Bring slowly to a boil. Adjust heat to a simmer.

Tie the bay leaf, parsley and celery leaves together, and add to the pot. Add onion, salt, pepper, potatoes and carrots. Place a loose-fitting lid on top and simmer 30 minutes.

Tie the leeks together, and add them to the pot. Add the fresh peas and simmer for 15 minutes, or until chickens and vegetables are tender. If frozen peas are used, follow the cooking-time instructions on the package.

To serve: Carve the chickens and place the pieces on a heated deep platter. Discard bay leaf, parsley, celery leaves and onion. Untie the leeks and arrange them attractively around the chicken pieces with the other vegetables. Skim the fat from the hot broth and pour 1 cup of broth over the chicken and vegetables. Garnish with parsley.

The broth may be seasoned to taste and served as a first course or refrigerated for future use.

Serves 6 to 8.

§ BOILED CHICKEN WITH GREEN OLIVES

Chicken, green olives and brown sugar—surely you will think it a strange marriage of flavors! However, I recommend you try it. It is delicious and can be prepared the day before it is to be served.

1 3- to 4-lb. chicken cut into serving pieces
1 medium onion, peeled
4 cloves
1 tsp. salt
½ tsp. paprika
1 tbs. brown sugar

5 cups basic stock or chicken stock from which all fat has been removed
2 tbs. butter
2 tbs. flour
1 2½ or 3 oz. bottle of pitted unstuffed green olives

Put the chicken pieces into a deep pot, add the onion stuck with the cloves, salt, paprika, brown sugar and stock. Bring to a boil. Place a loose-fitting lid on the pot, adjust the heat to a simmer and simmer 1 to 1½ hours, or until the chicken is tender.

When tender, lift the chicken pieces from the pot with a slotted spoon. Remove and discard the skin and bones, and cut the chicken meat into large pieces. Set aside.

Strain the stock into a bowl and skim off any excess fat. Pour the stock into a pot, and over a high heat bring it to a rapid boil and continue to boil, uncovered, until it is reduced to 2 cups.

Melt the butter in a small pot, and when foaming, add the flour and cook 2 minutes over low heat, stirring continuously. Add the 2 cups of hot stock, stir and cook until the sauce thickens.

Cut the olives into thin slices and add to the sauce. Taste before adding salt; the olives add considerable tartness. Simmer gently for 5 minutes. Add chicken pieces and simmer another 5 minutes.

To serve: Serve the chicken in the pot in which it was cooked or in a heated serving dish. Serve with rice or noodles.

Serves 4 to 6.

Note: Green olives stuffed with pimientos may be substituted for the unstuffed green olives.

§ BOILED CHICKEN SALAD

A dish to be served as a salad or as a first course.

1 2½- to 3-lb. chicken
1½ to 2 quarts basic stock or chicken stock from which all fat has been removed

3 generous slices fresh ginger root
2 tbs. lemon juice
5 to 7 tender young scallions, washed

Put the chicken into a deep pot, and add enough stock to barely cover it. Add the ginger and lemon juice. Place a lid on top and bring to a boil. Adjust the heat to a simmer, and simmer for 45 minutes, or until tender.

When tender, remove the pot from the heat and allow the chicken to cool in the stock.

When cool, remove the chicken. Strain the stock into a bowl and reserve for future use.

Cut away and discard all the skin from the chicken. Carve the chicken. Remove the meat from the pieces by tearing it with your fingers into thin shreds 2 to 3 inches long. Put the shreds into an attractive glass salad bowl.

Trim off the roots of the scallions and cut the tops lengthwise. Use only the part of the tops which is crisp, fresh and green. Cut them into 2-inch fine, thin slivers. Add to the shredded chicken and toss. Cover and place in the refrigerator to chill.

Make vinaigrette (see p. 178). Pour it over the chilled chicken and scallions, toss and serve.

Serves 6 to 8.

§ WHITE CHICKEN I

This is the classic French Poulet au Blanc, and it has, I am sure, as many variations as a hen has feathers. These two versions come from the recipe collection of an elegant French lady, the grandmother of a dear friend, who titled her handwritten book Recettes de Cuisine du "Bon Vieux Temps." The little book is a treasure, and I am pleased to include her recipes from "the good old days."

1 4- to 4½-lb. roasting chicken	2 cups cold water
2 quarts basic stock or chicken stock from which all fat has been removed	

Truss the chicken, place it in a deep pot and add the stock and water. Cover with a loose-fitting lid, and simmer over a low heat for 1½ to 2 hours, or until the chicken is tender.

When tender, remove the chicken to a heated platter and keep warm.

Skim off any excess fat from the stock and prepare the following white sauce:

4 tbs. sweet butter	2 egg yolks
4 tbs. flour	½ cup heavy cream
2 cups of hot stock in which the chicken was cooked	½ lb. fresh mushroom tops, thinly sliced
1 tsp. salt	1 tsp. lemon juice
⅛ tsp. cayenne pepper	Parsley, finely chopped

Melt the butter in a heavy pan over a low heat. Add flour, stir and blend 3 minutes; do not brown. Remove from heat and add the hot stock, salt and pepper. Stir briskly until smooth. Return to heat and stir continuously until the sauce comes to a boil. Stir and simmer gently 3 to 5 minutes.

In a bowl mix the egg yolks with the cream. Beat 1 cup of the hot sauce into the egg and cream mixture bit by bit. When well blended, add to the sauce, and stir and cook over a low heat until the yolks thicken it slightly.

When slightly thickened, add mushrooms and lemon juice. Cook and stir for 3 minutes. Do not boil.

To serve: Remove the skin from the chicken, carve the chicken into serving pieces and place them over a bed of fluffy white rice or cooked noodles. Spoon the sauce carefully over the chicken pieces and garnish with parsley.

Serves 6.

§ WHITE CHICKEN II

An exceptionally rich and nutritious dish, because all the chicken juices, as well as the fat, are absorbed into the vegetables. These succulent vegetables become the sauce.

1 3½- to 4-lb. chicken	1 bay leaf
Salt	2 cups celery stalks, including
Pepper	leaves, cut into 1-inch
Lemon wedge	pieces
2 medium carrots, scrubbed and	8 sprigs parsley
quartered	½ cup dry white wine
2 medium onions, peeled and	½ cup basic stock or chicken
thickly sliced	stock from which all fat
1 small white turnip, washed	has been removed
and thickly sliced	2 tsps. salt
1 clove garlic, peeled and cut	¼ tsp. pepper
in half	

Salt and pepper the inside of the chicken. Rub the outside with lemon. Truss.

Put all the vegetables and herbs in the bottom of a heavy pot. Add wine, stock, salt and pepper. Place chicken, breast side down, on the bed of vegetables. Place a tight lid on top and cook over a low heat 1 to 1½ hours, or until chicken is tender. Remove the chicken to a hot platter, keep hot and prepare the sauce as follows:

Discard the bay leaf. Put all the vegetables, together with the liquid, through a food mill, or blend in a blender until smooth. Pour into a sauce pan, correct seasoning, stir and bring to a boil.

To serve: Carve the chicken into serving pieces, arrange them on a heated platter and spoon the sauce over them. Serve with noodles or rice.

Serves 6.

§ *STUFFED CHICKEN IN THE POT*

And not nine days old! An unusual and good meal. Do not use an old fowl; be sure that your butcher gives you a fat, plump roasting hen.

1 4- to 5-lb. roasting hen
Lemon wedge
Chicken liver
Chicken gizzard and heart
2 cups coarse breadcrumbs
2 small cloves garlic, peeled and finely chopped
½ cup boiled ham, finely diced
1 tbs. parsley, finely chopped
½ tsp. pepper
1 tsp. salt
2 egg yolks
2½ quarts basic stock or chicken stock from which all fat has been removed
1 cup dry white wine
Watercress

Rub the chicken well inside and out with the lemon wedge.

Prepare the stuffing as follows: Boil the liver, gizzard and heart until tender, about 10 minutes. When tender, chop them and put them into a large bowl. Add the breadcrumbs, garlic, ham, parsley, pepper, salt and egg yolks. Mix thoroughly. Stuff the chicken. Sew up the openings of the chicken and truss.

Put the chicken into a deep pot and add the stock and wine. Bring slowly to a boil. Place a loose-fitting lid on top, adjust the heat to a simmer and simmer for 1½ to 2 hours, or until the chicken is tender.

When tender, carefully remove the chicken to a heated platter. Remove and discard the trussing string and skin.

To serve: Garnish with sprigs of watercress. Serve at once.

Serves 6.

Variations:

a) Add additional vegetables—carrots, peas and potatoes—to the pot, and serve them on the platter with the chicken.

b) Strain the stock, remove any excess fat, taste for seasoning and serve as a first course.

§ CHICKEN CACCIATORE

1 3- to 4-lb. chicken, cut into serving pieces
Seasoned flour
5 tbs. olive oil
1 large onion, peeled and coarsely chopped
1 large green pepper, coarsely chopped after discarding seeds and white ribs
1 medium clove garlic, peeled and finely chopped
2 tbs. celery leaves, coarsely chopped

1 cup fresh tomatoes, peeled and diced, or canned tomatoes
1 cup basic stock or chicken stock from which all fat has been removed
2 tsps. salt
½ tsp. pepper
1 cup mushrooms, including stems, sliced
2 tsps. lemon juice
1 tbs. parsley, finely chopped

Dredge the chicken pieces lightly with the seasoned flour.

Heat the olive oil in a heavy pot. When hot, add chicken pieces and brown. Remove from the pot and set aside.

Add onion to the pot and cook until transparent. Add green pepper, garlic and celery leaves, and stir and cook 3 to 5 minutes.

Replace the chicken pieces in the pot, add tomatoes, stock, salt and pepper. Cover with a tight-fitting lid, and simmer 30 to 40 minutes. Stir occasionally.

Wipe the mushrooms clean, slice and sprinkle them with lemon juice. Add them to the pot 10 minutes before you are ready to serve.

To serve: Serve directly from the pot, or arrange the chicken pieces on a heated platter and spoon the vegetables and sauce over them. Garnish with parsley.

Serves 6.

§ CHICKEN IN WINE AND CREAM

Quite a rich dish, but it is so delicious that one should forego counting calories.

2 tbs. butter
1 3½- to 4-lb. chicken, cut into serving pieces
18 small white onions, peeled
1 tsp. salt
½ tsp. pepper

1 cup basic stock or chicken stock from which all fat has been removed
3 cups dry white wine
½ lb. small fresh or frozen mushroom caps
3 cups heavy cream

Put the butter into a large heavy pot, and when foaming, add the chicken pieces, skin side down. Turn the heat down, cover the pot and cook gently for 10 minutes.

Add the onions, salt and pepper. Cover and cook for 20 minutes.

Add the stock and wine; cover and simmer for 30 to 40 minutes, or until the chicken is barely tender.

Add the mushroom caps; cover and simmer for 5 to 10 minutes.

Remove the chicken, onions and mushrooms to a heated serving dish and keep warm. Add the cream to the sauce and boil it rapidly, over a high heat, uncovered, until it is reduced by one-half. At this point the sauce should be thick and smooth. Stir occasionally.

To serve: Pour the sauce over the chicken, onions and mushrooms, and serve at once.

Serves 6.

§ *CHICKEN WITH CURRY SAUCE*

A *Madras curry powder is recommended for this recipe.*

1 cup flour mixed with 2 tsps. salt, 1 tsp. pepper and 2 tsps. curry powder

2 2½- to 3-lb. chickens, cut into pieces

3 tbs. butter

2 tbs. oil

1 large onion, peeled and finely chopped

2 tbs. of the flour used for dusting the chicken

4 tsps. curry powder

1 tsp. tomato paste

1 tsp. sugar

1 tsp. salt

½ tsp. pepper

3 cups basic stock or chicken stock from which all fat has been removed

1 medium clove garlic, peeled and finely chopped

¾ cup heavy cream

2 tbs. parsley finely chopped

Lightly dust the chicken pieces in the mixed flour. Heat the butter and oil in a deep, heavy pot until foaming, then add the chicken pieces and brown until golden. Do not let them overlap.

When the chicken pieces are brown, remove them to a plate, add the onion to the pan; stir and cook until transparent. Remove the pan from the heat and add the flour, curry powder, tomato paste, sugar, salt and pepper. Stir until blended. Add the stock slowly, stirring continuously, until the ingredients are well mixed. Add the garlic, return the pan to the heat and stir and cook the sauce until it comes to a boil. Replace the chicken pieces, cover, adjust the heat to a simmer and simmer 30 to 35 minutes, or until the chicken is tender.

When tender, remove the chicken with a slotted spoon or tongs to a heated serving platter and keep warm. Over a high heat bring the sauce to a rapid boil, and boil, uncovered, until it is reduced to 1½ or 2 cups. Skim any excess fat off the surface of the sauce. Lower the heat and add the cream; stir until blended, heat, but do not boil.

To serve: Spoon the sauce over the chicken pieces, and garnish with the chopped parsley. Serve with noodles or rice.

Serves 6 to 8.

§ *CHICKEN WITH BASIL*

A *dish that freezes so beautifully, I usually double the ingredients so that two meals are prepared with a single effort.*

2 tbs. butter
1 4-lb. chicken, cut into serving pieces
¼ cup scallions, chopped
½ clove garlic, peeled and finely chopped
½ cup dry white wine
¾ cup fresh tomatoes, peeled and diced, or canned tomatoes

½ cup basic stock or chicken stock from which all fat has been removed
4 leaves fresh basil, chopped, or 1½ tsp. dried basil
1 bay leaf
2 sprigs parsley
1½ tsp. salt
¼ tsp. pepper

Melt the butter in a heavy pan, and when foaming, add chicken pieces and brown on all sides. Remove the chicken and set aside. To the pan add the scallions, and cook quickly until soft; do not brown. Add garlic and wine. Stir and boil over a high heat, uncovered, until the liquid has been reduced by one-half.

To this liquid add the tomatoes, stock, basil, bay leaf and parsley. Simmer 5 minutes.

Put the chicken pieces into the sauce, add salt and pepper and cover tightly. Cook 25 to 30 minutes over a low heat, or until the chicken is tender.

To serve: Remove the bay leaf and parsley, put the chicken pieces into a heated serving dish and pour the sauce over them.

Serves 4 to 6.

§ *PARSLEY CHICKEN*

At *first glance this appears to be a variation of the Green Chicken Stew recipe given on p. 84. However, it is not even a first cousin! It freezes perfectly, but be sure to defrost it in a double boiler, not over direct heat.*

3 tbs. butter
1 3½- to 4-lb. chicken, cut into serving pieces
Salt
Pepper
Lemon
1 cup parsley, finely chopped

½ cup breadcrumbs
3 cups basic stock or chicken stock from which all fat has been removed
1 cup white wine
2 egg yolks
2 tbs. heavy cream

Melt the butter in a heavy pot. Turn heat off, and add a layer of chicken pieces. Sprinkle them with salt, pepper, a few drops of lemon juice, and cover with parsley. Add another layer of chicken pieces, then salt, pepper, lemon juice and parsley, until all the chicken and parsley have been used. Sprinkle the breadcrumbs on top. Add stock and wine. Bring to a slow boil, cover with a loose-fitting lid and simmer 35 to 45 minutes, or until chicken is tender.

When tender, remove the chicken with a slotted spoon to a warm platter and keep hot.

Boil the cooking liquid rapidly over high heat, uncovered, until reduced to about 3 cups. This should take 15 minutes.

Beat the egg yolks lightly in a bowl with the heavy cream, then add 1 cup of the hot liquid bit by bit, stirring constantly, until blended. Pour the egg yolk mixture into the cooking liquid, and simmer and stir for 2 or 3 minutes. Do not boil.

Place the chicken pieces in the sauce.

To serve: This dish should be cooked in an attractive copper or ironware pot, as it can be taken right from the stove to the table. Serve it with rice or noodles.

Serves 6.

§ CHICKEN TARRAGON

2 2½- to 3-lb. chickens
Salt
Pepper
4 tsps. dried tarragon leaves, or 8 tsps. fresh tarragon leaves, finely chopped

½ tsp. garlic, finely chopped
Lemon wedge
2 tbs. butter
1 tbs. vegetable oil
4 cups basic stock or chicken stock from which all fat has been removed

Lightly salt and pepper the inside of the chickens. Stuff each with equal amounts of tarragon and garlic. Truss. Rub the outside of each bird with lemon.

Put the butter and oil into a heavy pot, and heat until foaming. Place the chickens, breast side down, in the hot fat, and cook and turn until they are golden brown. Carefully control the heat so that neither the fat nor the chickens burn.

In a separate pot bring the stock to a boil. When the chickens are a golden brown, pour the hot stock over them. Bring to a gentle boil. Cover the pot with a tight-fitting lid. Adjust the heat to a simmer, and simmer for 45 minutes, or until tender. Remove the chickens to a heated dish and keep hot.

Prepare the following tarragon sauce:

4 tbs. butter	2 tsps. dried tarragon leaves, or
4 tbs. flour	2 tbs. fresh tarragon
1 tsp. salt	leaves, finely chopped
⅛ tsp. cayenne pepper	1 egg yolk
2 cups strained hot stock in	1 tbs. brandy
which the chickens were	½ cup heavy cream
cooked and from which any	Parsley or watercress
excess fat has been	
skimmed	

Melt the butter in a heavy saucepan, add flour, salt and pepper. Stir over a slow fire for 3 minutes. Do not brown. Turn off heat, and add the stock and the tarragon. Bring to a boil, and cook over a low heat 5 to 10 minutes, stirring constantly. Remove from heat.

In a small bowl mix the egg yolk with the brandy, and add 1 cup of the hot sauce bit by bit, stirring all the while. When mixed, pour into the sauce, and cook over a low heat for 3 or 4 minutes, stirring constantly. Add the heavy cream. Stir and heat. Do not boil.

To serve: Carve the chickens into quarters, and place them on a heated deep platter or gratin dish. Carefully spoon all the sauce over the pieces. Garnish with small bunches of parsley or watercress at each side. A teaspoon of finely chopped fresh tarragon over the sauce is an attractive addition. Serve at once.

Serves 6 to 8.

§ CHICKEN AND HERBS IN RED WINE

A recipe based on a chicken and red wine dish my husband and I ate in a French village, Cézanne, many years ago. I do not believe this recipe is a duplication of what we enjoyed, but I do believe it is good. You may omit or add herbs to your taste. The wine should be the best your budget will permit.

When the chicken is ready for serving, the outside is a dark burgundy color, almost black, and the meat is snow white and succulent.

1 clove garlic, peeled and finely chopped
3 tbs. celery leaves, coarsely chopped
4 sprigs parsley
1 large onion, peeled and coarsely chopped
1 medium carrot, scrubbed and diced
4 cloves allspice, crushed, or ½ tsp. ground allspice
2 bay leaves, crushed
2 medium slices fresh ginger root, or ½ tsp. powdered ginger

1 large pinch each of dried marjoram, oregano, rosemary, saffron, sage, tarragon, thyme and dill
1 tsp. salt
½ tsp. pepper
1 tbs. lemon juice
¾ cup hot olive oil
1 4½- to 5-lb. chicken, cut into serving pieces
Red burgundy wine
3 cups basic stock or chicken stock from which all fat has been removed

Place all the ingredients except the chicken, wine and stock in a large bowl. Mix thoroughly. Add the chicken pieces skin side down. Add just enough wine to cover the chicken. Place a tight cover on the bowl. Marinate for 6 hours or preferably overnight. Turn the chicken pieces 3 or 4 times. Do not refrigerate.

After the chicken pieces have been marinated, put them, together with the marinade, into a heavy pot and add the stock. Place a loose-fitting lid on top, and bring to a boil. Adjust heat to a simmer, and simmer for 40 to 50 minutes, or until the chicken is tender.

When tender, remove the chicken pieces to a dish and keep warm. Strain the broth into a bowl through a fine sieve or 2 pieces of cheesecloth placed over a strainer. Skim off the excess fat, and prepare the following Sauce Morgan:

3 tbs. butter
1 small onion, peeled and finely chopped
¼ tsp. garlic, finely chopped
1 tsp. tomato paste
2 tsps. potato flour

2 cups of the strained stock
¼ tsp. salt
1 tsp. guava jelly
2 cups finely sliced mushrooms
Lemon juice

Heat 1 tablespoon of the butter in a heavy pan, and when hot, add the onion and cook until transparent. Remove from heat; add the garlic, tomato paste and flour. Stir and mix thoroughly. Add stock, salt and jelly, and stir until blended. Place over a low heat, bring to a boil, stirring continuously, and simmer 5 to 10 minutes.

Heat the remaining butter in a pan, and when foaming, add the mushrooms. Sprinkle with a few drops of lemon juice, and cook over a high heat 3 or 4 minutes, stirring and tossing. Add to the sauce. Stir.

To serve: Place the chicken pieces on a heated serving platter, and spoon over 1 cup of the sauce; serve the balance in a heated sauce-boat. Serve with rice, preferably wild rice.

Serves 6.

§ STEAMED CHICKEN AND RUM

The combination of rum and chicken is a good one. In the tropics rum is used generously in cooking, and it was once used much more extensively in the American kitchen than it is today. I find it adds a subtle flavor to many dishes.

1 4-lb. chicken
Lemon wedge
Salt
Pepper
4 tbs. celery leaves, coarsely chopped
1 medium carrot, scrubbed and quartered

3 scallions, washed and coarsely chopped
1½ cups basic stock or chicken stock from which all fat has been removed
1 cup dark rum

Rub the inside and outside of the chicken with the lemon wedge. Sprinkle the inside with salt and pepper. Stuff it loosely with the vegetables. Truss.

Pour the stock and rum into a large pot. Place the chicken breast side down on a trivet, or rack, set over the liquid. The chicken should not touch the liquid. Place a tight-fitting lid on top, and bring to a boil. Adjust the heat to a simmer, and gently steam for 1½ to 2 hours, or until tender. Remove to a heated dish and keep hot. Strain the stock into a bowl and prepare the following Rum Sauce:

2 tbs. butter	1 pinch cayenne pepper
2 tbs. flour	2 cups of the hot stock
1 tsp. shallots, finely chopped	½ cup heavy cream
¼ tsp. garlic, peeled and finely chopped	2 tbs. rum
	2 tbs. parsley, finely chopped
½ tsp. salt	

Melt the butter in a heavy saucepan and add flour. Cook over a low heat for 3 minutes, stirring constantly. Add shallots, garlic, salt and pepper, and cook for 2 minutes. Remove from fire and add the hot stock. Cook slowly for 10 minutes, stirring all the while. Add the cream and rum. Stir. Heat, but do not boil. This should be a thin sauce.

To serve: Carve the chicken and remove the skin. Arrange the pieces attractively on a warm serving platter. Spoon over the chicken just enough of the sauce to coat it, and sprinkle it with the parsley. Serve the balance of the sauce in a heated sauceboat. Rice or noodles make a nice companion for this dish.

Serves 6.

§ STEAMED CHICKEN WITH RICE AND MUSHROOM STUFFING

1 4- to 5-lb. roasting chicken
Lemon wedge
2 tbs. butter
1 small onion, peeled and
finely chopped
1 tsp. salt
½ tsp. pepper
½ cup long-grain Carolina rice

1 cup mushrooms, including
stems, finely chopped
Lemon juice
½ tsp. thyme
½ cup dry white wine
1½ cups basic stock or chicken
stock from which all fat
has been removed

Rub the outside and inside of the chicken well with the lemon. Remove all pieces of excess fat and set aside.

Heat the butter in a heavy saucepan, add onion and cook until transparent. Do not brown. Add salt, pepper and rice. Stir continuously over a low flame for 5 minutes. Remove from heat and add mushrooms. Sprinkle with a few drops of lemon juice, add thyme and mix thoroughly.

Stuff the chicken loosely with the rice and mushroom mixture. Space must be allowed for the rice to expand. Sew up the cavities, and truss. Place the pieces of chicken fat over the back of the chicken.

Pour the stock and wine into a steamer. Place the chicken breast side down on a trivet, or rack, set over the liquid. The chicken should not touch the liquid. Place a tight-fitting lid on top. Bring the liquid to a boil, adjust the heat to a simmer and gently steam for 1½ to 2 hours, or until the chicken is tender.

Check the liquid in the steamer from time to time, and add more stock if necessary.

To serve: Untruss the chicken, place it on a bed of watercress on a large heated platter and surround it with steamed carrots and peas. Save the stock for future use.

Serves 6.

§ STEAMED BABY CHICKENS
Be certain that your butcher gives you the smallest birds.

3 1- to 1½-lb. baby chickens
Salt
Pepper
Sweet butter
3 cups dry white wine
2 cups basic stock or chicken
    stock from which all fat has
    been removed
Chicken gizzards and hearts,
    cut into small pieces

1 medium truffle, finely chopped
Stuffing:
  12 leaves fresh tarragon,
     chopped, or 1 tsp.
     dried tarragon
  1 medium clove garlic, cut
     into 3 pieces
  3 small carrots, scrubbed
     and cut into 1-inch
     pieces
  3 sprigs parsley

Sprinkle the cavities of the chickens with salt and pepper.

Mix the stuffing ingredients, and put an equal amount of it in each chicken. Generously rub the outside of each chicken with butter.

Put the wine, stock, chicken gizzards and hearts into the bottom of a steamer.

Place the chickens, breast side down, on a trivet, or rack, set over the liquid. The chickens should not touch the liquid. Place a tight-fitting lid on top. Bring the liquid to a boil, adjust the heat to a slow boil and steam for 1 to 1½ hours, or until the chickens are tender.

When tender, remove the chickens to a heated platter, and keep them warm.

Strain the stock into a bowl, and prepare a tarragon sauce (see pp. 77 and 117). Save any remaining stock for future use.

To serve: Cut the chickens in half. Remove strings and discard stuffing. Arrange the chickens on a heated platter and spoon the Tarragon Sauce over them. Garnish with the chopped truffle, and serve at once.

Serves 6.

§ BRUNSWICK STEW

An adaptation of an early American stew. The original recipe called for all of the sweet sun-ripened vegetables of the summer season. It was then, and is now, a hearty one-dish meal. With today's frozen vegetables it can be prepared in any season. Serve it with hot cornbread.

2 tbs. bacon fat
1 tbs. butter
1 3- to 4-lb. chicken, cut into serving pieces
2 tbs. brandy
2 cups basic stock or chicken stock from which all fat has been removed
2 cups fresh tomatoes, peeled and diced, or canned tomatoes
¼ cup dry white wine
2 onions, peeled and thinly sliced
½ tsp. garlic, peeled and finely chopped
1 medium leek, including the fresh green leaves, washed and thinly sliced
1½ tsps. salt
½ tsp. pepper
½ tsp. sugar
1½ cups fresh or frozen small lima beans
1½ cups fresh or frozen corn kernels
Celery leaves, coarsely chopped

Heat the bacon fat and butter in a heavy, large pot. When hot, add chicken; fry until golden brown on all sides. Remove to a plate. Discard fat. Replace chicken, and flame with brandy. Add stock, tomatoes, wine, onions, garlic, leek, salt, pepper and sugar. Stir. Cover with a loose-fitting lid, and simmer 1 to 1½ hours, or until chicken is tender.

When tender, remove the chicken from the pot. Discard the skin and bones, and cut the chicken into large pieces. Set aside. Skim any excess fat off the stock. Add lima beans and corn. Cook 30 minutes, or until vegetables are tender. Return the chicken pieces to the pot and heat.

Serve in a heated serving dish, and garnish with the celery leaves.

Serves 6 to 8.

§ GREEN CHICKEN STEW

Heed the recipe and use a tremendously large bunch of parsley so that the sauce will have a delicate green tint. I am a firm believer in and user of the blender, but I find this dish is better if a food mill is used.

2 4-lb. chickens, cut into serving pieces
3 cups basic stock or chicken stock from which all fat has been removed
1 large bunch of parsley, well washed and coarsely chopped
2 whole bunches of celery, washed and coarsely chopped

4 large leeks, washed, with the white parts coarsely chopped
3 slices of white toast
1 cup of dry white wine
2 tbs. salt
1 tsp. pepper
Cold water
2½ cups heavy cream
2 cups peas, fresh or frozen
1 cup of long-grain rice

Put the chicken pieces into a large pot. Add stock, parsley, celery, leeks, toast, wine, salt and pepper. Add enough cold water to cover. Bring to a boil. Place a loose-fitting lid on the pot, and simmer 1½ to 2 hours, or until chickens are tender.

When tender, remove the pot from the heat, and with a slotted spoon remove chicken pieces from the broth. Remove and discard the skin and bones from the chickens, and dice the meat into ½-inch cubes. Set aside.

Strain the stock into a bowl, and put the parsley, celery and leeks through a food mill. Set aside.

Skim any excess fat from the strained stock, and return it to the pot. Bring it to a rapid boil over a high heat, and boil, uncovered, until it is reduced to approximately 4 quarts.

Measure out 1 quart of the stock, and bring 3 cups of it to a boil, add the rice, cover and cook until tender.

Bring the remaining 1 cup of stock to a boil, add the peas, cover and cook until tender. If frozen peas are used, follow the cooking directions given on the package using stock instead of water.

To the remaining stock, approximately 3 quarts, add the puréed vegetables and diced chicken. Slowly bring to a boil, add cream and stir. Heat, but do not boil.

To serve: Pour the stew into a heated soup tureen. Put the peas and rice into two heated serving dishes. At the table ladle a portion of the stew into heated individual soup plates, and spoon into each dish 2 tablespoons of peas and a generous portion of rice.
Serves 8.

§ *CHICKEN MARENGO*

2 2½- to 3-lb. chickens, cut into serving pieces
Seasoned flour
3 tbs. butter
3 tbs. olive oil
2 ozs. brandy
1 tsp. garlic, peeled and finely chopped
1 bay leaf
 6 sprigs parsley

½ cup basic stock or chicken stock from which all fat has been removed
½ cup dry white wine
1½ cups fresh tomatoes, peeled and diced, or canned tomatoes
1 tsp. salt
¼ tsp. pepper
½ lb. small mushroom caps, or if large, thickly sliced
1 tbs. parsley, finely chopped

Dredge the chicken pieces lightly in the seasoned flour.

Put the butter and olive oil into a heavy pot, heat until foaming, add the chicken pieces and brown until golden all over.

Heat the brandy, and flame the chicken. Add the garlic, tie the bay leaf and parsley together and add them to the pot with the stock, wine, tomatoes, salt and pepper. Cover the pot, and simmer gently over a low fire for 30 to 40 minutes, or until the chicken is tender.

When tender, add the mushroom caps, or slices, stir and cook 3 to 5 minutes.

To serve: Remove the bay leaf and parsley. Serve in the pot in which it is cooked, or ladle into a heated casserole. Garnish with the chopped parsley.
Serves 6.

§ CHICKEN WITH WHITE ONIONS

To peel onions without tears, put the onions in a pan and pour boiling water over them. Leave for 10 seconds. Drain, and rinse under cold running water. Make a small cross at the root end of the onion, and the outer skin will slip off easily.

The dish can be frozen without loss of flavor, but do not put it over direct heat to reheat it. Place it in a double boiler over a medium heat. When it is piping hot, serve at once. Do not continue to cook.

¾ lb. butter
4 lbs. small white onions, peeled
3 2- to 2½-lb. chickens, quartered
4½ cups basic stock or chicken stock from which all fat has been removed

¼ cup dry white wine
1½ cups rice
3 tsps. salt
½ tsp. pepper
3 cups light cream
4 ozs. bourbon whiskey
1 tbs. parsley, finely chopped

Put the butter in the top of a double boiler, add onions, cover and cook over boiling water for 1 hour, or until tender.

Meanwhile, put the chicken pieces in a pot, and cover them with the stock and wine. Bring to a boil, adjust heat to a simmer and gently simmer for 25 to 30 minutes, or until tender. When tender, remove the chicken to a flameproof casserole and keep warm.

Measure the broth in which the chickens were cooked; it should be 4½ cups. If not, add additional stock. Bring to a boil, and add rice, salt and pepper. Cover and cook until the rice is tender.

When the onions are tender, pour them, together with the butter in which they were cooked, over the chicken. Add the cream and cooked rice. Carefully stir the ingredients together, heat over a low flame and add the bourbon. Stir and heat. Do not boil.

Garnish with the parsley, and serve at once.

Serves 6.

§ COLD CHICKEN WITH LEMON

A superb summer dish. It should be made a day in advance so that it can set properly and so that you and your kitchen can remain cool. Serve it with crisp watercress salad and a cold dry white wine.

1 3- to 4-lb. chicken, cut into serving pieces
Peel of ½ lemon
1½ to 2 quarts basic stock or chicken stock from which all fat has been removed

3 tbs. thin slivers of lemon peel
¼ cup lemon juice
¼ cup sherry
1 tsp. salt
2 egg yolks
1 cup heavy cream

Put the chicken pieces into a deep pot, and add the peel of half a lemon. Add the stock, which should barely cover the chicken. Bring to a boil. Cover with a loose-fitting lid. Adjust heat to a simmer, and simmer 1 to 1½ hours, or until the chicken is tender.

When tender, remove the pot from the heat. Let the chicken cool in the stock.

When cooled, remove the chicken and discard the skin and bones. Cut the meat into neat, small pieces. Set aside.

Remove any excess fat from the stock, and strain stock into a bowl. Pour the stock into a pan and boil rapidly, uncovered, until it is reduced to 1½ cups. Add 2 tablespoons of the slivered lemon peel, the lemon juice, sherry and the salt. Boil gently for 5 minutes.

In a bowl combine the egg yolks with the heavy cream, and add the hot sauce bit by bit, stirring continuously. When blended, put the mixture into the pot, and stir it briskly over a low heat for 3 or 4 minutes until it is slightly thickened. Add the chicken pieces. Mix.

Pour the mixture into an attractive glass dish and chill thoroughly for at least 4 hours, or preferably overnight. The sauce should have the texture and appearance of a custard.

To serve: Garnish with the remaining tablespoon of slivered lemon peel, and serve on individual chilled plates.

Serves 4 to 6.

§ CHICKEN BREASTS IN SOUR CREAM SAUCE

An easy party dish and one that can be made early and reheated, but if you reheat, do so over a very low heat, or preferably over hot water. Serve with rice.

6 whole chicken breasts, boned
Flour
4 tbs. butter
3 tbs. hot Marsala wine
2 tbs. flour
1 tsp. tomato paste
1 cup hot basic stock or
    chicken stock from which
    all fat has been removed
2 cups sour cream

2 tsps. salt
⅛ tsp. cayenne pepper
2 tsps. currant jelly
2 tbs. grated Parmesan cheese
¼ lb. mushroom caps
Lemon juice
1 tbs. sherry
1 tbs. fresh dill, finely chopped,
    or 1 tsp. dried dill

Dust the chicken breasts lightly with flour. Put 3 tablespoons of the butter into a heavy pot, and when foaming, add the breasts, skin side down. Brown quickly all over. Add the hot Marsala wine.

Remove the chicken breasts, lower the heat and add the flour and tomato paste. Mix well. Stir in the hot stock. Cook and stir until the sauce thickens. Add the sour cream slowly, stirring briskly all the while. Add salt, pepper, jelly and cheese. Stir. Replace the chicken breasts. Cover and simmer gently for 15 to 20 minutes, or until tender.

Cut mushroom caps into fine slices. Put the remaining tablespoon of butter into a pan with a few drops of lemon juice. When foaming, add the mushrooms, and cook over a high heat, stirring and shaking the pan, for 3 or 4 minutes. Add the sherry and dill. Stir. Add to the chicken breasts, and mix very gently. Heat, and serve in the pot in which the chicken was cooked, or place the chicken breasts on a heated platter and carefully spoon the sauce over them.

Serves 6.

§ CHICKEN TETRAZZINI

Another Italian classic, and so easy to prepare if you have a boiled chicken in the pot. It is a delicious one-dish meal that can be frozen and reheated in the oven. If you do freeze it, do not add the cheese and glaze until ready to serve.

2 cups boiled chicken meat	½ tsp. pepper
7 tbs. butter	¼ tsp. nutmeg
4 tbs. flour	1 canned red pimiento, finely diced
2 cups hot basic stock or chicken stock from which all fat has been removed	1 cup Parmesan cheese, grated
1 cup heavy cream	½ lb. thin spaghetti
2 tbs. sherry	1 tsp. lemon juice
2 tsps. salt	½ lb. mushrooms, finely sliced
	1 tbs. parsley, finely chopped

Remove skin from the chicken, and discard. Dice the meat into ½-inch cubes. Discard the bones.

Melt 4 tablespoons of the butter in a heavy saucepan. Add flour and cook, stirring constantly, 2 or 3 minutes. Do not brown. Add the stock. Stir and cook until it comes to a boil. Add cream, sherry, salt, pepper, nutmeg, pimiento and ½ cup of the cheese. Continue stirring, cook over a low heat for 3 or 4 minutes. Keep warm.

Cook the spaghetti in 3 quarts of salted boiling water until tender. When tender, drain and pour into a buttered serving dish. Mix in ¼ cup of the cheese and 2 tablespoons of the butter. Keep warm.

Meanwhile, sprinkle the lemon juice over the mushroom slices and sauté them in the remaining tablespoon of butter over a high heat for 3 or 4 minutes.

Scatter the chicken pieces and mushrooms over the top of the spaghetti, and pour the hot sauce over them. Sprinkle the remaining ¼ cup of cheese over the top, dot with butter and place under a broiler until the cheese has melted and the top is glazed.

Serve in the serving dish, and garnish with parsley.

Serves 6.

§ CHICKEN DADO

An interesting and delicious way to use the chicken that went into the preparation of your basic or chicken stock. Serve it with rice or noodles.

2 cups boiled chicken meat, diced
3 tbs. butter
3 tbs. scallions, finely chopped
1 cup water chestnuts, sliced
2 tsps. fresh ginger root, slivered
2 cups sour cream

½ cup basic stock or chicken stock from which all fat has been removed
2 tsps. salt
1 tsp. lemon juice
½ tsp. pepper
1 tbs. scallion tops, finely chopped

Discard skin and bones of chicken, and dice the meat into neat cubes.

Heat the butter in a heavy, large pot until foaming, add scallions and cook until soft. Do not brown.

Remove from the heat and add the water chestnuts, ginger, sour cream, stock, salt, lemon juice and pepper. Return to the heat and bring to a boil. Add chicken. Heat through, but do not cook. Stir gently and as little as possible so that the chicken pieces do not break up.

Serve immediately in a heated serving dish, and garnish with scallion tops.

Serves 6.

§ BOILED CHICKEN WITH DILL SAUCE

Another superb use for your boiled chicken. It can be prepared days in advance and frozen. If you do freeze it, do not add the cheese and glaze until it is defrosted and reheated.

1 3½- to 4-lb. boiled chicken
4 tbs. butter
4 tbs. flour
2 cups hot basic stock or chicken stock from which all fat has been removed
1 tsp. salt

1 pinch cayenne pepper
1 tsp. dried dill, or 3 tsps. fresh dill, finely chopped
1 egg yolk
½ cup heavy cream
2 tbs. grated Parmesan cheese

Remove skin from the chicken. Carve the meat into large serving pieces. Discard bones.

Butter individual casseroles or one large gratin dish, and place the chicken meat in the dishes or dish.

Melt the butter in a heavy saucepan. Add flour and cook, stirring constantly, 2 or 3 minutes. Do not brown. Add stock. Stir and cook until the mixture comes to a boil. Add salt, pepper and dill. Simmer 5 minutes.

In a small bowl mix the egg yolk with the heavy cream. Add 1 cup of hot sauce bit by bit, stirring rapidly, until blended. Pour slowly back into the sauce, and cook a minute or two, stirring constantly. Do not boil.

Spoon the sauce over the chicken pieces. Sprinkle with cheese, dot with butter and place under a broiler until the cheese has melted and the top is glazed. Serve at once.

Serves 4 to 6.

§ COLD HAM AND CHICKEN MOUSSE

This recipe is an elegant solution to the problem of what to do with leftover ham and chicken. Particularly good during the summer, it should be served with a chilled rosé or dry white wine.

Vegetable oil	1 tsp. tomato paste
1½ cups cooked ham, finely ground	1 pinch cayenne pepper
	¼ tsp. salt
1 cup cooked chicken meat, finely ground	2 egg yolks
	2 egg whites
1½ envelopes unflavored gelatin	1 cup heavy cream
¼ cup cold water	¼ cup sherry
1 cup basic stock, chicken stock or veal stock, clarified	1 large cucumber, washed and cut into paper-thin slices
	Sprigs of watercress

Lightly oil a 1-quart metal ring mold or loaf pan. Set aside.

The ham and chicken should be ground through the finest blade of the meat grinder, or cut into fine cubes and put through a blender. Set aside.

Soak the gelatin in the cold water. Bring the stock to a boil, add tomato paste, pepper and salt. Add the gelatin and stir until dissolved.

Beat the egg yolks lightly in a bowl, and add the stock bit by bit, stirring continuously. Return the mixture to the pan, and over a very low heat cook and stir until it coats the back of a wooden spoon. Remove from the heat and cool.

When cool, beat the egg whites until stiff, and fold and blend them into the stock mixture. Beat the cream until stiff, and fold and blend it into the mixture. Fold in the ham, chicken and sherry. Pour into the mold, cover and refrigerate until set.

To serve: Turn the mold out onto a chilled platter, and decorate with the cucumber slices and watercress.

Serves 6.

§ CHICKEN LIVER PÂTÉ

We find this marvelous for a picnic. If the pâté is well chilled in a thick covered crock, it will keep firm and cool for hours; that is, if the sun is not too hot!

14 tbs. butter	¼ tsp. salt
1 small onion, peeled and coarsely chopped	¼ tsp. nutmeg
	¼ tsp. mace
¾ lb. chicken livers	1 pinch cayenne pepper
¼ cup basic stock or chicken stock from which all fat has been removed	¼ tsp. anchovy paste
	1 tbs. brandy
½ tsp. dry mustard	½ tsp. lemon juice

Melt 3 tablespoons of the butter in a medium pot, and when foaming, add onion and cook and stir until transparent. Add chicken livers, stock and 4 more tablespoons of the butter. Stir and cook over a medium heat until the livers are tender, 15 to 20 minutes. Add the seasonings, anchovy paste, brandy, lemon juice and the remaining 7 tablespoons of butter. Put into a blender and blend until smooth, or press through a food mill.

Pour the mixture into a crock. Cover and chill.

To serve: Serve directly from the crock with plain toast squares or a good dark pumpernickel bread.

Serves 6.

Variation: Pâté in aspic (see recipe pp. 24–25): Cool the liver mixture, but do not let it become firm. Melt 1 cup of aspic, and pour it into the bottom of a lightly oiled metal mold. The aspic should be ¼ inch thick. Chill until set. Carefully pour and gently press the liver mixture over it. Cover and refrigerate until firm.

To serve: Unmold on a plate, and garnish with watercress sprigs.

§ DUCK IN RED WINE

A dish that can be made early in the day and reheated or frozen for future use.

If the dish is prepared early, there is time to chill the sauce in the refrigerator, and all the fat congealed on the surface can be removed effortlessly.

2 4-lb. ducks, cut into serving pieces	Red wine
1 tsp. salt	Seasoned flour
½ tsp. pepper	2 tbs. butter
¼ tsp. nutmeg	Livers of the ducks
2 medium onions, peeled and finely chopped	Gizzards and hearts of the ducks
1 clove garlic, peeled and finely chopped	6 sprigs parsley
½ cup brandy	1 bay leaf
½ cup basic stock or chicken stock from which all fat has been removed	2 stalks celery, cut into 2-inch pieces
	½ lb. mushrooms, including stems, coarsely sliced

Put the pieces of duck into a large bowl; add salt, pepper, nutmeg, onions, garlic, brandy and stock. Mix. Add sufficient red wine to cover the duck pieces. Place a tight-fitting lid on the bowl, and marinate 4 hours or overnight. Occasionally turn and move the pieces around so that each is well marinated.

When marinated, remove the duck pieces and dry thoroughly on paper towels. Do not discard the marinade. Dredge the duck pieces in the flour. Melt the butter in a large, heavy pot, and when hot, add the duck pieces and brown on all sides. Remove and set aside.

To the same pot add the liver, gizzard and hearts, and cook 10 or 15 minutes and then discard them. To this delicately seasoned fat replace the duck pieces and add the parsley, bay leaf and celery. Add the marinade. Cover and bring slowly to a boil. Adjust the heat to a simmer, and simmer for 1½ to 2 hours, or until the duck is tender.

When the duck is tender, remove it from the sauce and set aside. Strain the sauce into a metal bowl, and cool it as rapidly as possible in the refrigerator or freezer. When cool, remove it. Discard all the fat that has congealed on the surface.

Pour the liquid into an attractive serving pot, add the duck pieces and the mushrooms. Mix. Bring to a slow boil, and simmer for 10 minutes uncovered.

Serve with wild rice, white rice or noodles.

Serves 6.

§ STEAMED DUCK

If you enjoy duck but have been avoiding it because of its excessive fat, try this recipe, which is practically fat-free. The preparation entails quite a few steps, but it is not complicated, and the result is delicious. It can be prepared a day in advance and reheated without any loss of flavor or tenderness.

2 4- to 5-lb. ducks
  Lemon wedge
  Salt
  Pepper
½ cup crushed dried mushrooms, or 1 cup fresh mushrooms, finely chopped
2 carrots, scrubbed and quartered
2 stalks celery, cut in 2-inch pieces
1 orange, cut in quarters

2 small onions, peeled and coarsely chopped
6 medium slices fresh ginger root, or 1 tsp. powdered ginger
6 sprigs parsley
1 cup basic stock or chicken stock from which all fat has been removed
2 cups dry white wine
  Necks, gizzards and hearts of the ducks
  Watercress or parsley

Rub the ducks inside and out with the lemon wedge. Sprinkle the inside of each with salt and pepper. Stuff each duck with an equal amount of the mushrooms, carrots, celery, orange, onions, ginger and parsley. Truss the ducks.

Pour the stock and wine into the bottom of a large pot or a steamer. Add the neck, gizzards, and hearts. Set the livers aside for use in the sauce. Place a rack, or trivet, in the pot. It should be high enough so that the ducks do not touch the liquid. Place the ducks, breast side down, on the rack. Place a tight-fitting lid on top of the pot so that the ducks cook in a heavy bath of steam. Bring the liquid to a boil, turn the heat down and steam slowly for 1½ to 2 hours, or until the ducks are tender.

When tender, remove the ducks from the steamer. Cut off all the skin, but do not discard. Place the ducks in a covered container and refrigerate.

Place the skin of the ducks in a cake or bread pan, sprinkle with salt and put in a 350° F. oven. As the fat is rendered from the skin, pour it off. Continue cooking and pouring off the fat until the skin is crisp and deep golden in color. Remove from the oven, and drain on a double thickness of paper towels so that all excess fat is absorbed.

Strain into a bowl the stock over which the ducks were steamed. Refrigerate. When cool, remove and discard all fat congealed on the surface. Heat the stock and prepare the following orange sauce:

2 tbs. butter	½ tsp. salt
Livers of the ducks	¼ tsp. pepper
1 tsp. shallots, finely chopped	2 tsps. ginger root, finely slivered, or ¼ tsp. powdered ginger
¼ tsp. garlic, finely chopped	
1 tsp. tomato paste	
3 tsps. potato flour	½ cup Madeira wine
1½ cups of the hot stock	2 tsps. guava jelly
Peel from ½ an orange, cut into fine slivers	

Heat the butter in a heavy pan, and when foaming, add the livers and cook until brown on all sides. Remove and discard the livers. Remove the pan from the heat, and add the butter, the shallots, garlic, tomato paste and potato flour. Stir until thoroughly mixed. Add the hot stock, replace the pan over a low heat and cook, stirring continuously, until smooth. Add orange peel, salt, pepper, ginger, Madeira and jelly. Bring to a boil, and simmer slowly 5 to 10 minutes. Stir occasionally.

A half-hour before serving time assemble the dish as follows:

Cut away and discard the congealed fat from the ducks. Discard the stuffing. Carve the ducks.

Pour the remaining stock into the steamer. If it does not measure 1½ cups, add water or wine. Place the duck pieces on the rack of the steamer. They should not touch the liquid. Bring the liquid to a slow boil, cover with a tight-fitting lid and steam 15 to 20 minutes to reheat the duck pieces.

Place the golden, crisp skin in a warm oven to reheat. Heat the sauce.

To serve: Arrange the duck pieces attractively on a heated platter, and spoon 1 cup of the sauce over them. Crush 1 cup of the crisp skin, and sprinkle it over the ducks and sauce. Crush the balance of the skin, and serve it with the balance of the sauce in side dishes. Garnish the platter with sprigs of watercress or parsley.

Serves 6 to 8.

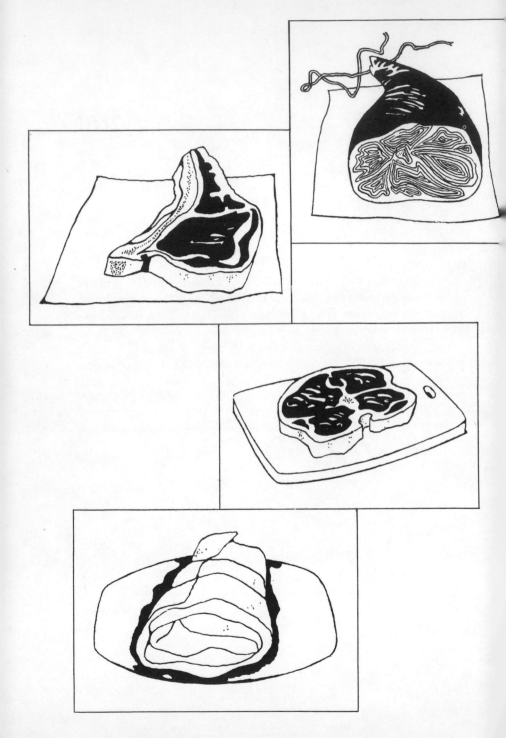

4 Meat

MEAT NOTES

CANNED BEEF STOCK or a bouillon cube may be used in the following recipes, but the result will not be as good as it will if you use your own stock.

Before serving a stew or meat sauce, skim off the fat. This is easily done by firmly gripping a side of the pot with one hand and tipping it away from you. With the other hand skim off the excess fat with a large spoon.

The leanest meats are always the best buy; use them.

Seasoned flour is 1 cup of flour combined with 2 teaspoons of salt and ½ teaspoon of pepper. Prepare 2 or more cupfuls and store in a closed container; in this way a supply is always available.

All pepper should be freshly ground.

Taste before you serve! Correct the seasoning to *your* taste.

§ BOILED BEEF

Truly one of the great dishes. I cook the potatoes separately because they tend to cloud the broth. However, if you prefer, they can be added to the pot with the carrots and onions.

Should any of the beef be left over, it is delicious sliced cold, cut into thin strips and added to a mixed salad, or cubed and added to a vegetable soup.

6 lbs. brisket of beef

3 quarts cold basic stock or beef stock from which all fat has been removed

2 lbs. small white onions, peeled

12 medium carrots, scrubbed and cut in half

2 lbs. small new potatoes, scrubbed, or 8 regular medium potatoes, peeled and cut in half

1 lb. peas, fresh or frozen

2 tbs. parsley, finely chopped

Put the brisket of beef into a large pot, add the stock and bring to a boil. Cover with a loose-fitting lid, adjust heat to a simmer and simmer for 1½ hours.

Add onions and carrots. Simmer for another hour. Add peas. If the peas are fresh, allow 15 to 20 minutes' cooking time; if frozen, 4 minutes' cooking time.

Steam the potatoes in a separate pot until tender, and keep warm. If small new potatoes are used, do not peel them as the skin is flavorful and nutritious.

When ready to serve, remove the beef and carve into thin slices against the grain. Arrange the slices neatly on a large heated platter. Surround the meat with the potatoes, carrots, onions and peas. Spoon ¾ cup of the hot broth over the meat and vegetables. Sprinkle the whole dish with the parsley.

Taste the broth and correct the seasoning. Serve it as a first course, or in cups together with the beef and vegetables. Serves 8.

Note: Many sauces such as dill, horseradish or mustard—are excellent with Boiled Beef but the most delicious, in my opinion, is the following Spring Sauce:

2 hard-boiled eggs	2 tsps. salt
2 slices white bread	1 tsp. pepper
¼ cup milk	1½ tbs. vinegar
1 egg yolk	1 tbs. lemon juice
3 tbs. salad oil	1 medium head Boston lettuce, washed and shredded
1 cup light cream	
1 cup sour cream	½ cup chives, finely chopped

Peel and chop the eggs. Cut off and discard the crusts of the bread. Cube the bread, put it into a small bowl, pour the milk over it and stir and soak until soft.

When the bread is soft, pour it into a large mixing bowl, add the chopped eggs and all of the other ingredients. Stir and mix thoroughly.

This is a thin sauce and should not be too piquant. If you want it to be more tart, add additional salt and lemon juice.

Serve it in a large glass bowl with a good-size ladle or serving spoon, as each person will want an ample helping.

§ *BOILED BEEF WITH VEGETABLE PURÉE*

3 lbs. brisket of beef	4 medium potatoes, peeled and cubed
4 cups basic stock or beef stock from which all fat has been removed	2½ tsps. salt
2 medium onions, peeled and sliced	1 tsp. pepper
	3 tbs. butter
4 medium carrots, scrubbed and sliced	2 tbs. parsley, finely chopped

Put the meat into a large pot, and add the stock. Bring to a boil, adjust heat to a simmer, cover, and simmer for 1½ hours. Add vegetables, 1 teaspoon of the salt and ½ teaspoon of the pepper, and continue simmering for 1 hour, or until the meat and vegetables are tender.

When tender, remove the beef to a plate and keep warm. Strain the vegetables, and reserve the broth for future use.

Put all the vegetables through a food mill or a blender with the butter, remaining salt and pepper, and just cnough broth—approximately 1 cup—to make a thick purée.

To serve: Slice the beef, and arrange the slices neatly on a warm platter; surround them with the puréed vegetables, and garnish with the parsley.

Serves 6.

§ BEEF IN RED WINE

If a burgundy wine is used in this recipe it is a Boeuf Bourguignon. However, any good dry, full-bodied red wine can be used. It is a splendid party dish and can be prepared 1 or 2 days in advance. It requires no last minute preparations; just reheat slowly.

8 slices bacon, cut into 1-inch pieces	1 bay leaf
2 tbs. bacon fat	1 pinch thyme
2 tbs. butter	1¼ tsps. salt
4 lbs. lean beef, top round or chuck, cut into 1- to 1½-inch pieces	½ tsp. pepper
	1 tsp. tomato paste
2 tbs. brandy	16 to 18 small white onions, peeled
1½ cups dry red wine	1 lb. mushrooms, including stems
1½ cups basic stock or beef stock from which all fat has been removed	3 tsps. potato flour
	3 tsps. cold water
1 carrot, peeled and finely sliced	2 tbs. parsley, finely chopped

Cook the bacon over a low flame in a deep heavy pot until most of the fat is rendered. Do not brown. Remove from the pot, and drain on paper towels. Discard all but 2 tablespoons of the bacon fat.

Add the butter to the bacon fat, and when hot, brown the pieces of beef. Do not let them overlap; as they brown remove them to a plate. When all are brown, return them to the pot and flame them with the brandy. Stir, and add the wine, stock, carrot, bay leaf, thyme, salt, pepper, tomato paste and bacon pieces. Bring to a boil, adjust the heat to a simmer, cover with a tight-fitting lid and simmer for 45 minutes.

Add the onions to the pot. Remove the stems from the mushrooms, and set the caps aside. Cut the stems into rings and add to the pot. Cover and simmer for 30 minutes, or until the beef is tender.

If the mushroom caps are small, add them whole; if large, slice them into thick slices and add them to the pot. Cover and cook 5 minutes.

Mix the potato flour with the cold water and add to the pot. Stir and cook until thickened. Remove the bay leaf, and garnish with parsley.

Serves 6 to 8.

§ BRAISED BEEF

The principal elements of this dish are a spicy marinade, good stock and a lean cut of beef. It can be prepared in advance and reheated.

4½ to 5 lbs. lean chuck, round or rump of beef
1 tbs. salt
½ tsp. pepper
2 medium carrots, washed and thinly sliced
1 large onion, peeled and thinly sliced
3 stalks celery, including leaves, coarsely diced
2 cloves garlic, peeled and coarsely chopped
2 tsps. thyme
1 bay leaf
1 whole clove
1 tsp. basil
2 tbs. parsley, finely chopped
3 cups red wine
¼ cup brandy
½ cup olive oil

Trim any excess fat from the meat, and rub it with salt and pepper. Mix all the ingredients in a large bowl, add the meat and turn it around so that all sides are saturated with the marinade. Cover tightly. Marinate for at least 6 hours at room temperature, or, if possible overnight. Turn the meat frequently. When marinated, proceed as follows:

4 tbs. bacon fat
1 cracked veal knuckle
¼ lb. bacon rind
1 cup canned tomatoes
3 cups basic stock or beef or brown stock from which all fat has been removed

10 medium carrots, peeled and quartered
25 to 30 small white onions, peeled
Parsley or watercress sprigs

Remove the meat from the marinade; dry it thoroughly. Heat the bacon fat in a deep, heavy pot. When hot, add the meat and brown on all sides. Pour the marinade over the meat, and add the veal knuckle, bacon rind, tomatoes and stock. Place a tight-fitting lid on top, adjust the heat to a simmer and simmer 3 to 4 hours, or until tender. Turn the meat from time to time.

Boil the carrots and onions as directed in the chapter on Vegetables (pp. 165 and 169).

When the meat is tender, remove it to a plate, strain the liquid into a large bowl and skim off the fat. Return the liquid to a clean pot, and boil it over a high heat, uncovered, until it is reduced to 4 cups. Add the meat, carrots and onions, and simmer for 5 minutes.

To serve: Carve the meat and arrange it neatly on a heated platter; surround it with the carrots and onions, and spoon 1 cup of the sauce over the meat and vegetables. Serve the balance of the sauce in a separate dish. Garnish with parsley or watercress sprigs. Serve with rice or boiled potatoes.

Serves 10 to 12.

§ POT ROAST

This is a basic pot roast. You can make it more elaborate by adding other vegetables—peas, turnips or string beans, for example—and your favorite combination of herbs. The vegetables should be added during the last hour of cooking. If you use frozen vegetables, when you add them to the pot roast, allow for the cooking time shown on the package.

4 lbs. chuck, round or rump of beef	½ cup red wine
1 clove garlic, peeled and cut in half	1 cup canned tomatoes
1 tbs. bacon fat	½ tsp. pepper
1 large onion, peeled and cut in thin slices	1½ tsps. salt
1 bay leaf	½ tsp. sugar
½ cup basic stock or beef or brown stock from which all fat has been removed	6 medium potatoes, peeled and cut in half
	6 medium carrots, scrubbed and cut in half
	2 tbs. parsley, chopped

Trim any excess fat from the meat. Rub well with the cut garlic. Tie the meat with a string so that it will hold its shape during cooking and so that it can be lifted easily to and from the pot without piercing it with a fork.

Heat the bacon fat in a large, heavy cast-iron pot. When hot, add the meat and brown on all sides. Remove to a plate.

Place a low rack (most cast-iron pots, which are also known as dutch ovens, come with a rack) in the bottom of the pot, and put the onion and bay leaf on it. Place the browned meat on top, and pour in the stock, wine and tomatoes. If the tomatoes are whole, cut them in small pieces. Add pepper, salt and sugar. Place a tight-fitting lid on top, adjust heat to a simmer and simmer for 1 to 1½ hours.

After this cooking period, the pot can be set aside. An hour before serving time, add potatoes and carrots, cover and return to a low heat for 1 hour, or until vegetables are tender.

To serve, place the meat on a heated platter and surround it with the vegetables. Discard the bay leaf. Skim off excess fat from the sauce, bring to a boil and pour the sauce over the meat and vegetables. Garnish with chopped parsley.

Serves 6.

§ BEEF STEW WITH GHERKINS

The addition of the gherkins and coriander give this familiar recipe an unusual and special touch.

3 tbs. vegetable oil
2½ to 3 lbs. lean chuck, cut into
    2-inch pieces
2 medium onions, peeled and
    coarsely chopped
3 tomatoes, peeled, seeded
    and coarsely chopped
1 tbs. tomato paste
3 cloves garlic, peeled and
    finely chopped
2 tsps. salt
½ tsp. pepper
⅛ tsp. coriander powder

1 cup basic stock or beef stock
    from which all fat has
    been removed
½ tsp. thyme
1 bay leaf
3 sprigs parsley
3 sprigs fresh dill, or ½ tsp.
    dried dill
6 medium potatoes, peeled
6 large carrots, peeled and
    halved
4 tbs. sour gherkins, finely
    chopped
2 tbs. parsley, finely chopped

Heat the oil in a heavy pot, and nicely brown the pieces of meat. Do not let them overlap, and as they brown remove them to a plate. When all the meat is browned, add the onions and stir and cook until transparent. Return the meat to the pot. Add the tomatoes, tomato paste, garlic, salt, pepper, coriander powder and stock. Tie up in a cheesecloth the thyme, bay leaf, parsley, and dill and add to the pot. Bring to a boil, stir and place a lid on top. Adjust the heat to a simmer, and simmer for 1½ hours.

Add the potatoes and carrots, and cook for 40 minutes, or until tender. Add the gherkins and stir.

Serve the stew in the pot in which it is cooked, or ladle it into a heated serving dish. Garnish with the chopped parsley.

Serves 6.

§ SWISS STEAK WITH SOUR SAUCE

The sharpness of the sauce goes well with boiled potatoes or rice. Add a green salad and your dinner is ready.

2 tsps. salt	1½ cups basic stock or beef
½ tsp. pepper	stock from which all fat
3 tbs. flour	has been removed
3 to 4 lbs. top round steak	3 tbs. wine vinegar
¼ cup vegetable oil	2½ tsps. prepared mustard
3 medium onions, peeled and	1 bay leaf
thinly sliced	Parsley

Mix the salt and pepper with the flour, sprinkle it onto both sides of the steak and rub it in.

Heat the oil in a heavy pot, and brown the steak well on both sides. Lower the heat, add the onions and cook until transparent. Add the stock, vinegar, mustard and bay leaf. Bring to a boil, adjust the heat to a simmer, place a tight-fitting lid on top and simmer for 2 hours, or until tender.

To serve, remove the bay leaf. Place the steak on a heated platter; spoon the sauce over the meat. Garnish with sprigs of parsley. Serves 6.

§ GROUND BEEF AND NOODLES

2 tbs. vegetable oil	1 6-oz. can tomato paste
1 tbs. butter	2 tsps. salt
2 medium onions, peeled and	½ tsp. pepper
thinly sliced	1 bay leaf
2 lbs. lean ground round or	½ lb. medium wide noodles
chuck beef	1 cup sour cream
3½ cups basic stock or beef	1 tbs. fresh dill, finely
stock from which all fat	chopped, or 1 tsp. dried
has been removed	dill

Melt the oil and butter in a heavy, large pot, and when hot, add the onions. Cook until transparent. Add the beef, breaking it up into small pieces. Cook and stir until slightly browned. Add stock, tomato paste, salt, pepper and bay leaf. Bring to a boil, add noodles and stir. Adjust heat to a simmer, cover, and simmer for 25 to 30 minutes, or until noodles are tender.

When tender, remove the bay leaf and add the sour cream and dill. Heat, but do not boil.

To serve: Serve directly from the pot in which it was cooked, or pour into a covered heated serving dish.

Serves 6.

§ *STEAMED SPICED BEEF*

This is tender, spicy and delicious hot or cold. It can be prepared in the morning and reheated without any loss of flavor. The origin of this recipe is Venezuelan.

3½ to 4 lbs. bottom round of beef	1 slice bacon, cut into ½-inch pieces
Vegetable oil	8 small green olives with pimiento stuffing, halved
Salt	½ clove garlic, peeled and cut into thin slivers
Pepper	Watercress or parsley
Prepared mustard	

Trim excess fat off the beef. Using a sharp, pointed knife, slash many small holes in the beef, then rub it with oil, salt, pepper and mustard. Into each slash insert a piece of the bacon together with a sliver of garlic and half an olive. Tie the meat up with a string, and put it into a bowl with the following marinade:

1 cup basic stock or beef stock
from which all fat has
been removed
2 cups dry red wine
½ cup olive oil
1 clove garlic, peeled and quartered
2 medium onions, peeled and
sliced
2 carrots, scrubbed and sliced

2 shallots, peeled and cut in
quarters
1 bay leaf, crushed
1 clove
3 sprigs parsley
7 peppercorns
2 tsps. salt
3 juniper berries
4 tsps. soy sauce
1 pinch basil
1 pinch thyme

Cover the bowl tightly, and marinate the beef for 3 hours or, if time permits, overnight. Turn the beef occasionally.

When ready to cook, remove the meat to a plate. Pour the marinade, together with spices and vegetables, into a pot. Place a rack, or a trivet, over the liquid. On the rack place the following vegetables:

1 carrot, scrubbed and thinly
sliced
1 medium onion, peeled and
thinly sliced

8 sprigs of parsley
4 stalks of celery, coarsely cubed

Put the meat on top of the vegetables, and cover with a tight-fitting lid. Bring the liquid to a simmer, and steam for 1 to 2 hours. One hour's cooking time will give you rare beef; two hours' cooking time will give you well done meat.

When cooked to your taste, remove the meat to a heated platter. Strain the marinade into a saucepan, and boil it rapidly uncovered, over a high heat, until it is reduced to 2 cups.

Remove the string from the meat, and carve it in medium-thin slices. Arrange them attractively on the heated platter. Spoon a few tablespoons of the sauce over the sliced meat, and serve the balance in a sauceboat. Garnish with watercress or parsley.

Serves 6 to 8.

§ STEAMED VEAL AND PORK PUDDING

This pudding is delicious hot or cold; if it is to be served cold, omit the sauce. The pudding can be made in the morning, left in the mold and reheated over steam prior to serving. Since the sauce too can be made in the morning, this is a good dish to serve when company is coming.

Butter
2 tbs. butter
1 medium onion, peeled and finely chopped
2 lbs. ground lean veal
¾ cup ground lean pork
2 cups fine bread crumbs
4 egg yolks
2½ tsps. salt

½ tsp. pepper
½ tsp. paprika
2½ tbs. parsley, finely chopped
¼ cup heavy cream
1 cup basic stock, chicken or veal stock, from which all fat has been removed
4 egg whites
Watercress or parsley sprigs

Generously butter the inside of a 2-quart metal mold, including the inside of the lid.

Melt the 2 tablespoons of butter in a small pan, and when foaming, add the onion and cook until transparent. Do not brown.

Put in a large bowl the veal, pork, bread crumbs, egg yolks, salt, pepper, paprika, parsley, cream and stock. Add the onion together with the butter in which it was cooked. With your hand, mix the ingredients thoroughly until blended.

Beat the egg whites until stiff, and with a wooden spoon, work one-third of them into the meat mixture. Fold in the balance, and pour into the prepared mold. Cover and steam (see Steaming Directions, p. 186) for 2½ hours.

Prepare the following brown sauce:

2 tbs. butter
2 tbs. flour
½ small onion, peeled and finely chopped
½ tsp. tomato paste

1½ cups basic stock or brown stock from which all fat has been removed
½ tsp. salt
¼ tsp. pepper
1 tsp. currant jelly

Heat the butter in a small saucepan until foaming. Add the flour and onion, and stir and cook until both are brown. Remove from the fire. Add tomato paste, stock, salt, pepper and jelly, and stir until blended. Return to the fire, and stirring continuously, cook until the sauce has thickened, about 10 minutes. When thickened, strain into a bowl and discard the onion pieces. Return the sauce to a pan and heat.

To serve: Turn the pudding out onto a heated platter, spoon the sauce over it, and garnish with watercress or parsley sprigs.
Serves 6 to 8.

Variation: Wash and finely dice ¼ lb. mushrooms. Add them to the sauce, and cook for 3 or 4 minutes.

§ VEAL CHOPS CREOLE

Serve these chops and the rich sauce with rice, boiled potatoes, or noodles.

1 tbs. butter
2 tbs. olive oil
6 large veal chops, lightly dusted with seasoned flour
1 medium onion, peeled and finely chopped
2 small cloves garlic, peeled and finely chopped
1 medium green pepper, its seeds and white membranes removed, cut into 2-inch strips
½ lb. mushrooms, including stems, cleaned and coarsely sliced

4 canned whole tomatoes, diced
1 small can tomato paste
2 tbs. parsley, finely chopped
1 bay leaf
½ tsp. sugar
½ tsp. rosemary
1½ tsps. salt
1 tsp. pepper
3½ cups basic stock or chicken or veal stock from which all fat has been removed

Heat the butter and oil in a deep pot. When hot, add the chops, and cook until golden brown on each side. Do not let them overlap.
Remove the chops to a plate, and add the balance of the ingredients to the pot. Stir and bring to a boil. Place the chops in

the sauce, adjust heat to a simmer, cover, and simmer for 1 hour, or until the chops are tender.

To serve: Remove the bay leaf, place the chops on a heated platter, and spoon the sauce over them.
Serves 6.

§ *VEAL CHOPS ITALIANO*

A delicious party dish that can be cooked in advance and reheated without any loss of flavor or tenderness. To complete the menu, serve with a tossed green salad, a fresh loaf of rye bread and a dessert of chocolate mousse or a Bavarian cream. A rosé wine is a lovely compliment to the veal and its sauce.

6 thick veal chops
  Vegetable oil
2 tbs. butter
1 medium onion, peeled and sliced
1 small clove garlic, peeled and finely chopped
2 carrots, scrubbed and sliced
2 medium potatoes, peeled and sliced

1 cup basic stock or chicken stock from which all fat has been removed
2 cups canned tomatoes
½ tsp. rosemary
2 tsps. salt
½ tsp. pepper
  Parsley, finely chopped

Rub the veal chops with vegetable oil. Melt the butter in a heavy pot. Add the veal chops, and brown them well on each side. Place over them the onion (separate the rings as you add them to the pot), garlic, carrots and potatoes. Pour in the stock and tomatoes. If the tomatoes are whole, cut them in small pieces. Add rosemary, salt and pepper. Place a tight-fitting lid on top, turn the heat to low and simmer for 40 minutes, or until tender.

Serve directly from the pot, or put the veal chops in a heated gratin dish and spoon the vegetables and liquid over them. Garnish with parsley.
Serves 6.

§ VEAL WITH SAUSAGE

*If Italian sweet sausages are not available, use plain pork sausage.
This dish can be frozen.*

1 tbs. vegetable oil
1 tbs. olive oil
1 medium onion, peeled and thickly sliced
2 lbs. veal shoulder, cut into 1-inch cubes
½ lb. sweet Italian sausages, cut into 1-inch pieces
1 cup canned tomatoes

1½ cups rice
3 tbs. parsley, finely chopped
4 cups basic stock, chicken stock or veal stock from which all fat has been removed
1½ tsps. salt
½ tsp. pepper
3 tbs. Parmesan cheese, grated

Heat the oils in a deep pot, and when hot, add onion, veal and sausages. Stir and cook 5 minutes over a medium-high heat.

Add tomatoes, rice, parsley, stock, salt and pepper. Stir and bring to a boil. Cover, adjust heat to a simmer and simmer for 35 to 45 minutes, or until the meat is tender. Add cheese. Stir and cook for 5 minutes.

To serve: Pour into a heated serving dish.
Serves 6 to 8.

§ VEAL PAPRIKA

2½ lbs. leg of veal, cut into 2- to 3-inch pieces
¼ cup seasoned flour
3 tbs. butter
1½ tbs. olive oil
2 medium onions, peeled and thinly sliced
1½ tbs. paprika

2 cups basic stock or chicken stock or veal stock from which all fat has been removed
2 tbs. lemon juice
½ tsp. salt
¼ tsp. pepper
1 cup sour cream
2 tbs. parsley, finely chopped

Dredge the veal pieces in the seasoned flour. Heat 2 tablespoons of the butter and the olive oil in a deep, heavy pot. When hot, add the veal pieces in a single layer; do not let them overlap, and brown them on all sides. As the pieces brown, remove them to a plate.

After the veal is browned, add the remaining tablespoon of butter and the onions. Separate the rings as you put them into the pot. Cook until transparent. Add paprika, stir and pour in the stock. Put the veal pieces back into the pot. Add lemon juice, salt and pepper. Adjust heat to a simmer, cover with a loose-fitting lid and simmer for 1 hour, or until veal is tender.

Just before serving, add the sour cream, stir thoroughly and reheat. Do not boil.

To serve: Serve directly from the pot, or spoon into a heated serving dish. Garnish with the parsley.

Serves 6.

§ VEAL WITH MUSHROOM SAUCE

This is a relative of the famous French Veal Blanquette. I find it every bit as delicious and less work. One step that is eliminated is the skimming of the veal stock. The residue from the veal bones and meat does not discolor the sauce, and the nutriments contained in these tiny particles enrich the sauce.

Use a large pot to boil the veal and bones. You will have an ample quantity of a rich stock left over. If you use this in an aspic or a consommé, it should be clarified.

The marrow should be removed from the bones; it can be sliced and added to the sauce or, while it is hot, spread on crackers and eaten by the cook as a special treat.

4 to 4½ lbs. leg of veal
    Basic stock or chicken stock
    from which all fat has been
    removed (approximately
    2 quarts)

20 to 24 small white onions, peeled

Have the butcher remove the meat from the bones and cut the bones into 4- to 6-inch pieces. The meat can be left in large pieces.

Put the meat and bones into a large pot. Cover them by ½ inch with stock. Bring to a boil, cover with a loose-fitting lid and adjust the heat to a simmer. Simmer 1½ hours, or until the meat is tender.

While the meat is cooking, boil the onions (see p. 169), but do not discard their juices.

When the meat is tender, remove it with a fork, or tongs, to a cutting board. Strain the stock into a bowl and set aside. Cube the veal into 1- to 2-inch pieces, discarding any skin or tough gristle, and set aside.

Prepare the following mushroom sauce:

4 tbs. butter	1 tsp. salt
5 tbs. flour	¼ tsp. pepper
5 cups of the stock in which the veal was cooked and from which the fat has been removed	1 lb. mushrooms
	1 tbs. lemon juice

Melt the butter in a heavy saucepan, and when foaming, add the flour. Cook and stir continuously over a low flame for 3 minutes. Remove from the heat and add the stock, salt and pepper. Stir rapidly until the mixture is blended. Return to the heat, stir and simmer over a low flame for 5 minutes.

Clean the mushrooms and remove the stems (save them for the stockpot or a stew). If the caps are larger than 1 inch in diameter, cut them into coarse slices. Add them to the sauce together with the lemon juice and stir. Simmer uncovered for 5 minutes.

Put the cubed veal and the onions with all their juices into a flameproof serving casserole, and pour the mushroom sauce on top.

This dish may be set aside at this point, and the final step prepared as follows just before serving:

Bring the dish to a simmer over a low heat, and add the following:

3 egg yolks	1 tbs. parsley, finely chopped
1 cup heavy cream	¼ tsp. nutmeg
2 tbs. brandy	

Lightly beat the egg yolks with the cream and brandy. Stirring and folding continuously, slowly pour the egg-yolk mixture into the veal. Stir gently and heat. Do not boil. Garnish with the parsley and nutmeg, and serve at once. Serve with rice, noodles or new potatoes.

Serves 6 to 8.

§ VEAL WITH TARRAGON AND MUSHROOM SAUCE

If you cook the veal early it can be quickly reheated in the stock, or steamed. Caution: Reheat, do not cook. The sauce, too, can be prepared and reheated over hot water.

This dish is attractive served on a large platter surrounded with timbales of saffron rice. Use the extra veal stock for cooking the rice.

3½ to 4 lbs. sirloin of veal
2 cups basic stock, veal stock
  or chicken stock from
  which all fat has been removed
2 cups cold water
1 carrot, scrubbed and sliced
1 medium onion, peeled and
  sliced

1 clove garlic, peeled and
  sliced
1 stalk celery, cut into 1-inch
  pieces
2 whole cloves
1 bay leaf
½ tsp. dried tarragon
7 peppercorns
1 tsp. salt
½ cup dry white wine

Have the butcher roll and tie the veal securely with string. Put it into a deep pot, and add the stock and cold water, which should barely cover the veal. Add additional stock or water if necessary. Bring slowly to a boil, and add all the other ingredients. Bring back to a boil, adjust the heat to a simmer, cover and simmer for 1 hour and 45 minutes, or until the veal is tender when tested with a fork. Remove from the heat, and prepare the following tarragon and mushroom sauce:

2¼ tsps. dried tarragon, or ¼ cup fresh tarragon leaves, finely chopped
2 tbs. brandy
4 tbs. butter
4 medium mushrooms, including stems, cleaned and finely chopped
1 tsp. lemon juice
4 tbs. flour

1 tsp. salt
1 pinch cayenne pepper
1 pinch nutmeg
2 cups of the stock in which the veal was cooked, strained
1 cup heavy cream
3 egg yolks
2 tbs. light cream

Soak the tarragon in 1 tablespoon of the brandy and set aside.

Melt the butter in a small, heavy sauce pot, and when foaming, add mushrooms and lemon juice. Stir and cook for 3 minutes, remove from heat and add flour, salt, pepper, nutmeg and the veal broth. Stir until well blended. Return to heat and cook, stirring continuously until sauce comes to a boil. Stir and simmer gently 3 to 4 minutes. Add the heavy cream. Stir and heat.

Mix the egg yolks in a bowl with the remaining tablespoon of brandy and light cream. Beat 1 cup of the hot sauce into the egg mixture bit by bit. When blended, add to the sauce and cook over a low heat until the yolks thicken it slightly. Add the tarragon together with the brandy in which it was soaked.

To serve: Remove the strings from the veal, and slice it very thin. Arrange the slices neatly on a heated platter, and spoon the sauce over them.

Serves 6 to 8.

§ VEAL SHANKS IN TOMATO SAUCE

Ask your butcher for shanks with generous pieces of meat on them, and have him cut the bone into 2- to 2½-inch pieces. This dish freezes perfectly.

Flour
4 veal shanks, including their meat
2 tbs. oil
2 tbs. butter
3 medium carrots, scrubbed and finely diced
1 large onion, peeled and finely chopped
1 medium clove garlic, peeled and finely chopped
1 bay leaf, crushed
1 cup tomato sauce

2 tbs. tomato paste
1½ cups basic stock, chicken stock or veal stock from which all fat has been removed
1 tsp. salt
½ tsp. pepper
1 tsp. fresh ginger root, finely diced, or ¼ tsp. powdered ginger
1 cup white wine
Parsley, finely chopped

Flour the shanks lightly. Heat the oil and butter in a large pot. When hot, add the shanks, and cook until golden on both sides.

Remove the shanks to a plate, and add the carrots and onion. Stir and cook until the onion is transparent. Add the garlic, bay leaf, tomato sauce, tomato paste, stock, salt, pepper, ginger and wine. Stir and bring to a boil. Replace the shanks, adjust the heat to a simmer, cover, and simmer for 1½ hours, or until tender.

To serve: Place the shanks in a large heated gratin or serving dish, remove the bay leaf, and spoon the sauce over them. Garnish with parsley.

Serves 6.

§ OSSO BUCO

You should use a big pot or two medium pots so that all the succulent, marrow-filled bones are able to simmer freely in the sauce.

4 veal shank bones, including their meat
½ cup seasoned flour
4 tbs. olive oil
4 tbs. butter
½ tsp. sage
1 tsp. rosemary
1 large onion, peeled and finely chopped
1 clove garlic, peeled and finely chopped
2 medium carrots, scrubbed and finely diced

2 stalks celery, including leaves, washed and finely diced
1½ tsps. salt
½ tsp. pepper
1½ cups dry white wine
1½ cups basic stock or chicken stock from which all fat has been removed
3 tbs. tomato paste
2 tbs. parsley, finely chopped
1 clove garlic, peeled and finely chopped
1 tbs. grated lemon peel

Have your butcher cut and saw each shank into 3 pieces.
Thoroughly coat the veal pieces with the seasoned flour.

Heat the olive oil and butter in a large pot, or equal parts of both in two pots. When hot, add the veal pieces and brown until golden on all sides. Do not overlap the pieces while browning. When brown, remove to a plate and discard half of the fat in the pot.

Return the veal pieces to the pot. Sprinkle with sage, rosemary, onion, garlic, carrots, celery, salt and pepper. Place a tight-fitting lid on top, and braise over a high heat for 7 minutes.

Remove the lid and add the wine, stock and tomato paste. Stir. Replace lid, turn heat down to a simmer and simmer for 2 hours, or until tender.

Combine the parsley, garlic and lemon peel.

When ready to serve, place the veal pieces in a large heated serving dish, pour the sauce over them and sprinkle the top with the mixed parsley, garlic and lemon peel.

Serve with rice or noodles.

Serves 6 to 8.

§ CALVES' LIVER IN WINE SAUCE

12 slices bacon
1½ lbs. calves' liver, cut into 6
   thin slices
Flour
2 tbs. butter
2 medium onions, peeled and
   thinly sliced

1 cup basic stock or chicken
   stock from which all fat
   has been removed
½ cup dry red wine
½ tsp. salt
¼ tsp. pepper
1 pinch mace
Parsley sprigs

Fry the bacon until crisp. Set aside and keep warm. Discard all but 2 tablespoons of the bacon fat.

Remove any skin or membrane from the liver, and lightly dust the pieces with flour.

Put the butter and the 2 tablespoons of bacon fat into a large frying pan, and when hot, add the pieces of liver and cook until brown on each side. Allow 3 to 4 minutes to each side. Remove the liver to a heated serving platter, and keep warm.

Add the onions to the pan in which the liver was cooked, and stir and cook until transparent. Add the stock, wine, salt, pepper and mace. Bring to a boil over high heat, stirring continuously, and boil until the liquid is reduced to 1 cup.

To serve: Spoon a portion of the onions and sauce over each slice of liver, place the bacon slices around the edge of the platter, and garnish with a few sprigs of parsley. Serve at once.

Serves 6.

§ LAMB STEW

A change from the traditional spring lamb stew; in fact, I would call it an "all seasons" stew. It can be prepared a day or two in advance, and it can be frozen.

1 lb. white kidney beans
2½ lbs. boneless lamb, neck,
    shoulder or shank
2 ozs. butter
1 medium onion, peeled and
    coarsely chopped
4 tbs. flour
4 cups basic stock or beef
    stock from which all fat
    has been removed

1 carrot, scrubbed and cut in
    half
1 stalk celery, washed and cut
    in half
4 sprigs parsley
1 clove garlic
1 bay leaf
1 tsp. thyme
2 tsps. salt
½ tsp. pepper
2 tbs. parsley, finely chopped

Soak the beans 6 hours or overnight. Drain. Put them in a pot, cover with cold water and bring to a boil. Adjust heat to a simmer, and simmer for 30 minutes uncovered. Drain.

While the beans are cooking, trim any excess fat from the lamb and cut into 2-inch pieces.

Melt the butter in a deep pot, and when hot, add the meat and onion. Stir and cook until slightly browned. Sprinkle with the flour, and continue cooking, stirring continuously, until brown. Add the stock and stir. Add the beans. Make a *bouquet garni* by tying in a cheesecloth bag, or with a string, the carrot, celery, parsley, garlic and bay leaf, and add to the pot. Add the thyme, salt and pepper. Cover with a loose-fitting lid, and simmer for 2 hours.

To serve: Discard the *bouquet garni*. Ladle the stew into an attractive heated serving dish, and sprinkle with parsley.

Serves 6.

§ LAMB SHANK STEW

This dish can be frozen, but I prefer to freeze it before adding the vegetables, because cooked potatoes, which are such a succulent part of this dish, tend to lose flavor and texture in freezing. So I suggest the meat be frozen in its sauce. When you want to serve it, defrost, add the vegetables and continue to cook as directed.

6 to 8 lamb shanks
Flour
2 tbs. bacon fat
1 tbs. vegetable oil
2 tbs. brandy
1 large onion, peeled and
coarsely chopped
1½ tsps. tomato paste
1 clove garlic, peeled and
finely chopped
2 stalks celery, diced, including the leaves
1 bay leaf
½ tsp. thyme
2 tsps. salt

½ tsp. pepper
2½ cups basic stock or beef
stock from which all fat
has been removed
16 small white onions, peeled
8 medium carrots, peeled and
halved
8 medium potatoes, peeled
and halved, or 16
small new potatoes,
washed
1 cup fresh peas, or 1 box
frozen peas
2 tbs. parsley, finely chopped

Have the butcher cut the shanks into 2- to 3-inch pieces. Remove and discard any excess fat from the meat.

Lightly flour the shanks. Heat the bacon fat and oil in a large pot, and brown the shanks until golden. Remove to a plate.

Heat and flame the brandy, and pour it into the pot and deglaze. Add the onion, and stir and cook until transparent. Add the tomato paste, garlic, celery, bay leaf, thyme, salt, pepper and stock. Stir.

Return the lamb shanks to the pot. Bring to a boil, cover with a loose-fitting lid, adjust the heat to a simmer and simmer for 1 hour. Add the onions, carrots and potatoes, and continue to cook for 40 minutes. If fresh peas are used, add them and continue to cook until the vegetables are tender. If frozen peas are used, follow the cooking time as indicated on the package.

To serve: Remove the bay leaf, and serve the stew in a large heated tureen. Garnish with the parsley.

Serves 6 to 8.

§ *IRISH LAMB STEW*

A 6- to 7-quart pot is needed for this fine stew, which can be prepared a day in advance. Serve it with a green salad, a bottle of red wine and warm French bread.

4 lbs. boneless shoulder of lamb cut into 2- to 3-inch cubes

4 cups basic stock or beef stock from which all fat has been removed

4 cups cold water

½ cup red wine

8 medium potatoes, peeled

3 medium onions, peeled and coarsely sliced

4 leeks, washed and coarsely sliced, including the fresh green tops

4 stalks celery, washed and cut into 2-inch pieces

2 cloves garlic, peeled and sliced

¼ tsp. cayenne pepper

5 tsps. salt

6 medium carrots, peeled and cut into quarters

24 small white onions, peeled

2 tbs. parsley, finely chopped

Wash and trim excess fat from lamb cubes. Put the lamb into a deep large pot; add stock, water and wine. Cube 4 of the potatoes, and add to the pot together with the onions, leeks, celery, garlic, pepper and 3 teaspoons of the salt. Cover with a loose-fitting lid, and slowly bring to a boil. Stir. Adjust heat to a simmer, and simmer for 1 hour.

With a slotted spoon remove the pieces of lamb to a 5-quart pot. Strain the stock into a bowl, and set aside.

Purée the cooked vegetables through a food mill, or blend in a blender until smooth. Pour the purée over the lamb. Add the remaining 4 potatoes cut into quarters, the carrots, white onions and the remaining 2 teaspoons of salt.

Remove and discard the fat from the stock. Add 1 quart of the stock to the lamb and vegetable mixture. Stir. Cover and simmer over a low heat for 1 hour, or until the vegetables are tender.

To serve: Serve in the cooking pot, or ladle into a heated covered serving dish. Garnish with the parsley.

Serves 8.

§ LAMB IN WINE SAUCE

A delicious Sunday or company dish. It can be made in advance up to the point of reducing the sauce, and this is easily done at the last moment.

3 lbs. boneless lamb, shank,
shoulder, or neck, cut
into 1- to 2-inch pieces
3 tbs. butter
1 tbs. oil
2 tbs. brandy
2 medium onions, peeled and
finely chopped
2 tbs. tomato paste
½ medium clove garlic, peeled
and finely chopped
2½ tbs. flour

2 tsps. salt
½ tsp. pepper
2 cups basic stock or chicken
stock from which all fat
has been removed
½ cup dry white wine
1 bay leaf
1 cup heavy cream
½ lb. mushrooms, cleaned and
coarsely sliced
Lemon juice
Parsley

Trim any excess fat from the meat, and dry thoroughly. Heat 2 tablespoons of the butter and the oil in a deep, heavy pot, and when foaming, add pieces of the meat; do not overlap. Brown on all sides, and remove to a plate. Flame the brandy and pour it into the pan, stir and deglaze all the bits of brown crust. Add the onions and cook until transparent. Remove the pot from the fire, and add the tomato paste, garlic, flour, salt, pepper, stock and wine. Stir until blended. Add the bay leaf, and return the meat to the sauce. Bring the sauce to a boil, adjust the heat to a simmer, cover and cook for 1 hour, or until the meat is tender.

When tender, remove the meat with a slotted spoon to a heated serving platter, and keep warm. Remove and discard the bay leaf. Add the cream, stir and rapidly boil the sauce uncovered over a high heat until sauce is reduced to 2 cups.

Heat the remaining tablespoon of butter in a small pan, add a few drops of lemon juice, and when foaming, add the mushrooms. Cook and stir 2 or 3 minutes, and add to the sauce.

To serve: Spoon the sauce over the lamb, and garnish with the parsley. Serve with noodles, rice or boiled potatoes.

Serves 6.

§ LAMB WITH BROCCOLI

1½ tbs. butter
1½ tbs. vegetable oil
3 lbs. boneless shoulder of
   lamb, cut into 2-inch
   cubes
2 large onions, peeled and
   coarsely chopped
2 cups basic stock or chicken
   stock from which all fat
   has been removed

1 tsp. salt
½ tsp. pepper
2 bunches fresh broccoli,
   washed, or 2 boxes frozen
   broccoli
4 tsps. potato starch
Juice of 2 lemons
2 eggs

Heat the butter and oil in a heavy pot; add the lamb and brown. Add the onions, and stir and cook until transparent. Add the stock, salt and pepper. Cover, and simmer for 45 minutes. Add the broccoli, cover and cook until it and the meat are tender.

Dissolve the potato starch in the lemon juice, and add to the stew. Stir and cook for 3 to 5 minutes. Remove from heat.

Beat the eggs lightly in a bowl. Add 1 cup of the sauce from the stew to the eggs bit by bit, beating continuously. Add to the stew, stir and heat until thickened. Do not boil.

To serve: Pour into a heated serving dish.
Serves 6.

§ LAMB CHOPS WITH CAPERS

2 tbs. vegetable oil
3 tbs. butter
6 shoulder lamb chops
1 large onion, peeled and finely
   sliced
½ lb. mushrooms, thickly sliced
2 tbs. flour
1 tsp. tomato paste

1 cup dry white wine
½ cup basic stock or beef stock
   from which all fat has been
   removed
2 tbs. capers
1 tsp. salt
½ tsp. pepper

Heat the vegetable oil and 1 tablespoon of the butter in a large skillet, add the lamb chops and brown on each side. Do not overlap, and as the chops brown remove them to a plate. Discard the fat in which they are browned.

Melt the remaining 2 tablespoons of butter in a deep casserole, and when foaming, add the onion and mushrooms. Cook until the onion is transparent. Remove from the heat, and add the flour and tomato paste; stir until blended, and add the wine, stock, capers, salt and pepper. Return to the heat, and stir and cook until the sauce comes to a boil. Put the browned lamb chops into the sauce, cover, and simmer 35 to 45 minutes, or until the chops are tender.

To serve: Place the lamb chops on a heated serving platter, and spoon the sauce over them.

Serves 6.

§ *BOILED LEG OF LAMB*

Have your butcher do the boning and tying of the lamb. And don't forget to ask him to include the bone, which you can freeze and use in your stockpot.

½ cup butter
3½ to 4 lbs. leg of lamb, boned and rolled
2¾ cup of basic stock or beef stock from which all fat has been removed
4 carrots, scrubbed and sliced
18 small white onions, peeled
½ tsp. rosemary
  Bay leaf

3 tomatoes, peeled, seeded and quartered
1 cup dry white wine
1 small clove garlic, peeled and finely chopped
¼ cup canned tomato sauce
1 tsp. salt
½ tsp. pepper
1 tsp. sugar
1 tbs. fresh dill, finely chopped

In a heavy pot or Dutch oven melt the butter, and when foaming, add the lamb and brown on all sides. When brown, add one-quarter cup of the stock, the carrots, onions, rosemary and bay leaf. Cover tightly, and simmer over a low heat for 45 minutes.

Add the tomatoes, wine, garlic, tomato sauce and the remaining stock. Bring to a boil, cover tightly, and adjust heat to a simmer. Simmer for 1 hour, or until the lamb is tender.

When tender, remove the lamb to a heated platter and keep warm. Remove and discard the strings from the lamb. With a slotted spoon, or tongs, place the onions around the lamb. Skim the fat from the top of the sauce. Remove and discard the bay leaf. Add salt, pepper and sugar. Over a high heat reduce the sauce to approximately 2 cups. Put the sauce through a food mill or blend in a blender until smooth. Return the sauce to the pot, bring to a boil and spoon it over the lamb. Garnish with the dill and serve.

Serves 6.

Note: The lamb may be neatly carved in thin slices before serving, and a few tablespoons of the sauce spooned over the slices. The balance of the sauce should be served in a side dish.

§ BRAISED PORK CHOPS

I have suggested the chops be accompanied by a wine apple-sauce. This is a delicately seasoned sweet-sour sauce that is excellent with roast pork too.

1 tbs. vegetable oil
6 thick pork chops
2 large onions, peeled and thinly sliced
1 medium green pepper, with the white membranes and seeds removed, cut into thick slices

1 cup basic stock or beef or brown stock from which all fat has been removed
1½ tsps. salt
½ tsp. pepper

Heat the oil in a large, flat skillet, and when hot, add the pork chops and brown on both sides. Remove to a plate. Add the onions and green pepper to the pan. Stir and cook until the onions are golden. Add the stock, salt and pepper. Return the pork chops to the pan, and bring the liquid to a boil. Cover, adjust heat to a simmer and simmer for 45 minutes, or until the chops are tender.

To serve: Place the pork chops on a heated serving platter, and spoon the gravy, onion and green pepper over them. Serve with the following:

WINE APPLESAUCE:

4 tbs. butter
4 tsps. shallots, peeled and
    finely chopped
3 cups unsweetened plain
    applesauce

4 tbs. dry white wine
½ cup sugar
½ tsp. salt
⅛ tsp. pepper

Melt the butter in a small pot, and when foaming, add the shallots. Cook and stir over a low heat until soft. Do not brown. Add applesauce, wine, sugar, salt and pepper. Stir and bring to a boil. Simmer, uncovered, for 5 minutes. Serve in heated individual bowls.

Serves 4 to 6.

Note: If a sweetened applesauce is used, omit the sugar and add 1 additional tablespoon of wine.

§ SAUSAGES AND ENDIVES HUGUETTE

You don't need a large pot for this recipe. It is prepared on top of the stove, and because it is so delicious, I include it with my list of recipes. It was given to me by a French friend, who inherited it from her grandmother. It may be a first course, or the main course for a light supper or luncheon.

12 endives
12 small breakfast sausages
 5 tbs. butter
 2 tbs. olive oil
½ tsp. salt

¼ tsp. pepper
Basic stock or chicken stock
from which all fat has been
removed

Cut the endives in half lengthwise. Carefully hollow out the center of each half to make space for one sausage. Place the sausage in the center. Reshape the endives, and tie them up at each end with string.

Heat the butter and oil in a large, heavy frying pan. Put the endives in the pan side by side. Sprinkle with salt and pepper. Cook them over a slow fire, uncovered, turning occasionally, so that they can brown evenly all over.

Allow 30 to 40 minutes to braise them. The juices produced by the endives should be enough liquid, but if not, add a splash of stock so that they do not stick to the pan.

To serve, place on a heated platter and remove strings. Serve 2 to a person.

Note: The breakfast sausage is a small sausage approximately 2 inches in length.

§ PORK AND GREEN PEPPERS

Another delicious recipe from a French friend. It is a simple dish, and if you add the potatoes, it makes a whole meal. The green peppers can be frozen in their sauce and reheated. To reheat, place the pot over hot water or in a slow oven.

6 medium green peppers, washed	1 tsp. pepper
1 cup water	1 egg
¼ cup long-grain white rice	1 tbs. flour
3 tsps. salt	1 6-oz. can tomato paste
2 tbs. vegetable oil	2 tsps. sugar
1 large onion, peeled and finely chopped	3 cups basic stock or beef stock from which all fat has been removed
1 lb. lean pork, ground	1 tbs. parsley, finely chopped

Cut the stem end off the green peppers. Remove core, seeds and membranes. Be careful not to break the forms.

Bring the water to a boil, add the rice and ½ teaspoon of the salt. Cover and cook for 10 minutes only. Rinse under cold water, and drain thoroughly.

Heat in a pan 1 tablespoon of the vegetable oil, and when hot, add onions and cook until transparent.

Put into a mixing bowl the ground pork, the remaining 2½ teaspoons of salt, pepper, egg, partially cooked rice and cooked onions. Mix thoroughly with your hand. Stuff the pepper forms loosely with the mixture.

Put the remaining 1 tablespoon of vegetable oil and flour into a saucepan. Stir and cook over a medium heat until the flour is golden. Remove from the fire, add tomato paste and sugar, blend until smooth. Add stock, and stir until blended.

Place the stuffed green peppers upright in a heavy pot. Pour the sauce around them; it should come up to about three-quarters of the sides of the peppers. Place a tight-fitting lid on top, and bring to a boil. Adjust the heat to a simmer, and simmer for 50 to 60 minutes.

To serve: Remove the peppers carefully with tongs or a slotted spoon, and place them on a heated serving dish. Spoon part of the sauce neatly over the top of the peppers, and pour the balance around them. Sprinkle with parsley and serve.

Serves 6.

Variation: Peel 6 medium-size potatoes, add them to the pot and cook with the peppers in the tomato sauce.

§ SMOKED PORK AND BEANS

To cook 2 meals in one, double the amount of beans. Serve half of the beans with the pork, and refrigerate the balance for a cold bean salad, or reheat and serve later in the week with a tomato sauce. An economical—and nutritious—dish.

2 cups dried white kidney or
   Great Northern beans
3 cups basic stock or ham stock
   from which all fat has been
   removed
1 medium onion, coarsely
   chopped
2 tsps. salt

1 tsp. pepper
3 tbs. fresh celery leaves, finely
   chopped
Cold water
2 lbs. smoked boneless pork butt
   (Porkette)
1 tbs. scallions or parsley, finely
   chopped

Soak the beans in cold water overnight. Drain. Put them in a heavy pot, and add the stock, onion, salt, pepper and celery leaves. Add enough cold water to cover the beans by two inches.

Bring to a boil, cover, adjust the heat to a simmer and simmer for 45 minutes. Add the pork butt, replace cover and simmer for 1½ hours. Add additional stock if needed.

To *serve:* Ladle the beans into a heated deep platter or gratin dish. Carve the pork butt into ¼-inch slices, and overlap them down the center on top of the beans. Garnish with the scallions or parsley.

Serves 6 to 8.

§ SMOKED PORK CHOPS WITH LENTILS

The pork chops should be cut thick and be as freshly smoked as possible. Only a green salad and a fruit dessert are needed to complete the menu. The chops can be frozen.

2 lbs. lentils	1 medium onion, peeled
3 cups basic stock or ham stock from which all fat has been removed	2 tsps. salt
	8 smoked pork chops
	2 tbs. flour
Cold water	1 tsp. vinegar
1 bay leaf	½ cup sour cream
2 carrots, scrubbed	

Read the instructions on the lentil package, and if they are the "quick-cooking" variety, proceed with the recipe. If not, soak the lentils overnight, drain off the water and proceed as follows:

Put the lentils into a large pot, add the stock and cold water to cover by two inches; add bay leaf, carrots, onion and salt. Bring to a boil, cover with a loose-fitting lid and turn the heat down to a simmer. Simmer for half an hour.

Add pork chops and additional cold water to cover all the ingredients by two inches. Bring the pot back to a boil, adjust heat to a simmer, replace lid and cook for 1 hour.

Remove bay leaf, carrots and onion.

In a small bowl mix the flour with cold water until it is smooth. Add a little of the hot liquid from the lentils, beat until blended and slowly pour the mixture into the pot, stirring continuously.

Stir gently; do not mash the lentils. Add vinegar and simmer for 20 minutes.

When ready to serve, add the sour cream, stir and bring to a boil.

Serve in the pot in which it was cooked, or ladle into a heated, covered serving dish.

Serves 6 to 8.

§ AFRICAN RICE

A full meal, needing only a salad and dessert as complements.

1 lb. small pork sausages	2½ cups water
1 lb. cooked ham	2 cups basic stock or ham
3 large leeks	stock from which all fat
1 tbs. olive oil	has been removed
2 cups uncooked long-grain	2 tsps. salt
rice	1 tsp. pepper

Cut the sausages into ½-inch pieces. Cut the ham into small cubes. Set aside.

Wash the leeks thoroughly, and cut the white parts into thin slices and set aside. Do not use the green tops (save them for your stockpot).

Heat 1 teaspoon of the olive oil in a frying pan. Add the sausages and cook until brown. Set aside.

Heat the remaining 2 teaspoons of olive oil in a deep, heavy pot, and add the rice. Stir continuously with a wooden spoon over a medium heat until the rice is coated with the oil. Do not brown.

Add to the rice the sausages, ham, leeks, water, stock, salt and pepper. Bring to a boil, stir, cover with a tight-fitting lid and cook over a low flame 25 to 30 minutes, or until the rice is tender.

Serve directly from the pot.

Serves 6 to 8.

§ HAM WITH MADEIRA SAUCE

Either boiled or baked ham can be used in this recipe. It is an excellent way to use the remains of a baked ham.

2 tbs. butter
2 tbs. shallots, peeled and
    finely chopped
2 tsps. flour
1½ tsps. tomato paste
2 cups basic stock or ham
    stock from which all fat
    has been removed

2 tbs. Madeira
2 boxes frozen chopped spin-
    ach, or 3 cups fresh spin-
    ach, cooked, chopped and
    thoroughly drained
1 tsp. lemon juice
12 thin lean slices of cooked
    ham

Melt 1 tablespoon of the butter in a saucepan, add shallots and flour. Cook and stir until the flour is golden. Remove from the heat, and stir in the tomato paste; add the stock slowly, stirring continuously. Return the sauce to a low heat, and simmer slowly, uncovered, until the sauce is reduced to 1½ cups. Stir in the Madeira.

If frozen spinach is used, cook according to the directions on the package. Drain thoroughly. Put the cooked spinach into a saucepan over a low heat, stir in the lemon juice and keep warm.

Put the remaining butter into a pan, and heat the ham slices; do not brown.

To serve: Make a bed of the spinach on a heated serving platter or in gratin dish, overlap the ham slices neatly on top and spoon the sauce over them. Serve at once.

Serves 6.

§ CREAMED HAM AND MUSHROOMS

Eighteen minutes is the complete preparation time!

4 tbs. butter
2 tbs. flour
1½ cups chicken stock, ham
    stock or basic stock from
    which all fat has been re-
    moved
¼ tsp. pepper

3 cups cooked ham, diced into
    ½-inch cubes
½ lb. mushrooms, coarsely
    chopped
½ tsp. lemon juice
½ cup heavy cream

Melt 2 tablespoons of the butter in a sauce pot, add flour and stir and cook until blended. Remove from heat and add stock and pepper, stir until smooth. Return to heat, and stir and simmer for 5 minutes. Set aside.

Melt the remaining butter in a skillet, and when foaming, add ham, mushrooms and lemon juice. Stir and cook until slightly golden. Add to the sauce, stir and simmer for 5 minutes. Add heavy cream, heat, but do not boil.

To serve: Pour into a heated serving dish and serve with noodles or rice, or spoon over toast triangles on individual serving plates. Serves 6.

§ HAM CASSEROLE

This dish freezes well and is a full hearty meal in itself. Serve it with a mixed green salad and a loaf of rye bread.

Taste before adding any salt to the casserole, as the ham and stock may season it sufficiently.

1 8-oz. package of thin
  noodles
1 tbs. vegetable oil
1 tbs. butter
1 large onion, peeled and
  finely chopped
3 tbs. flour
1 cup milk
2 cups ham stock, chicken
  stock or basic stock from
  which all fat has been removed

½ tsp. pepper
2 cups cooked ham, diced
  into ½-inch pieces
1½ cups mushrooms, thinly
  sliced
2 tsps. scallions, finely
  chopped, including the
  fresh green leaves

Cook the noodles according to the directions on the package.

Meanwhile, heat the oil and butter in a deep, heavy pot. Add the onion, and cook until transparent. Remove from heat; stir in flour. Add milk and stock slowly, stirring constantly. Return to heat, stir and cook until the liquid comes to a boil. Add pepper, and simmer, uncovered, for 5 minutes. Add ham and mushrooms,

stir and simmer for 10 minutes. Add the cooked noodl
have been thoroughly drained. Stir and bring to a boil.

To serve: Serve in the pot in which it is cooked, or pour
heated serving dish, and garnish with the scallions.

Serves 6.

§ SZÉKELY GOULASH (HUNGARIAN)

*Another Székely goulash recipe! Yes, and the best you have ever
eaten. It is the family recipe of a well-known Hungarian artist,
Lazslo Fircha, now living in Venezuela. The paprika should be
the imported variety, if possible. Serve the goulash with boiled
potatoes, a cucumber salad and beer.*

2 tbs. vegetable oil
1 tbs. butter
2 medium onions, peeled and finely chopped
2 tbs. paprika
2½ lbs. pork ribs, including the bones, cut into 2- to 3- inch pieces
3½ cups basic stock or beef stock from which all fat has been removed

2 lbs. sauerkraut
1 pinch cumin powder
2 green peppers, with the core, seeds and white membranes removed, cut into 1-inch pieces
1 large tomato, peeled and chopped into coarse pieces
½ cup flour
¾ cup cold water
1 cup sour cream

Heat the oil and butter in a large, heavy pot; when hot, add the
onion. Stir and cook until golden. Add paprika and stir. Add pork
ribs and 1 cup of the stock. Stir and bring to a boil, cover, adjust
the heat to a simmer and simmer for 45 minutes.

Put the sauerkraut in a colander, rinse well with cold water and
add to the pork mixture. Also add the cumin, peppers, tomato
and the remaining 2½ cups of the stock. Stir and bring to a boil,
cover, adjust the heat to a simmer and simmer for 30 minutes.
Give it an occasional stir.

Mix and beat the flour with the cold water until it is a smooth liquid. Add it slowly to the pork and sauerkraut, stirring all the while. When well blended, simmer uncovered for 10 minutes.

When ready to serve, add the sour cream, stir and blend. Serve directly from the pot, or ladle the goulash into a heated serving dish.

Serves 6 to 8.

§ STUFFED ZUCCHINI ETTA

A splendid summer dish when the fresh, fat zucchini come out of your, or your neighbor's, garden. Select the larger zucchini for this recipe.

Should any of the stuffing be left over, roll it into small balls, and cook them in the sauce with the zucchini.

1 piece of white bread from which the crust has been removed
¼ cup sour cream
½ lb. lean beef, ground
¼ lb. lean veal, ground
¼ lb. lean pork, ground
2 tbs. onion, peeled and finely chopped
½ tsp. garlic, peeled and finely chopped

⅛ tsp. thyme
2 tsps. salt
½ tsp. pepper
1 egg
3 to 4 lbs. zucchini
2 tbs. olive oil
2 cups tomato sauce
1 cup basic stock or beef stock from which all fat has been removed
1 bay leaf
2 tbs. parsley, finely chopped

Cut the bread into small cubes, and soak them in the sour cream.

Put into a mixing bowl the beef, veal, pork, onion, garlic, thyme, salt, pepper, egg and soaked bread. Mix thoroughly with your hand.

Wash the zucchini. Cut off each end, and with a grapefruit knife or a long spoon, remove the center seeds and core. Stuff the hollow center with the meat mixture.

Put into a heavy pot the olive oil, tomato sauce, stock and bay leaf. Place the zucchini side by side in the sauce, and bring to a boil. Adjust the heat to a simmer, place a tight-fitting lid on top and simmer for 40 to 50 minutes.

To serve: Remove the zucchini from the sauce and cut into 2-inch-wide diagonal slices. Arrange the slices attractively on a heated platter. Remove and discard the bay leaf. Spoon the sauce over the slices of stuffed zucchini and sprinkle the parsley over the top. Serves 6.

§ *MIXED MEATS GISEL*

¾ lb. bottom round or shank of beef
¾ lb. shoulder of veal
¾ lb. shoulder or shank of lamb
4 medium carrots, peeled and finely diced
2 medium leeks, white parts only, washed and thinly sliced

4 tbs. parsley, finely chopped
1 tbs. vegetable oil
1 tsp. salt
½ tsp. pepper
¼ tsp. thyme
¼ cup basic stock or beef stock from which all fat has been removed

Trim any excess fat from the meat. Cube into ½-inch pieces. Mix together.

Combine the carrots, leeks and parsley.

Heat the oil in a heavy pot, and when hot, add a layer of the meat pieces, cover with a layer of the combined vegetables and continue with the layers until all the meat and vegetables are in the pot. Sprinkle with salt, pepper and thyme, and pour in the stock. Place a tight-fitting lid on top, lower the heat to a simmer and simmer for 30 to 40 minutes.

Serve over a bed of rice or noodles.
Serves 6.

§ SWEDISH MEATBALLS

If you want to add a special touch, soak the bread in heavy cream instead of light cream. This dish freezes perfectly, but add the sour cream and herbs just before serving.

4 slices white bread, trimmed and cubed
¾ cup light cream
1 tbs. bacon fat
1 small onion, peeled and finely chopped
1 lb. lean beef, ground
½ lb. lean pork, ground
½ lb. lean veal, ground
3 eggs
½ tsp. garlic, finely chopped
½ tsp. nutmeg

3 tsps. salt
1 tsp. pepper
4 tbs. butter
1 tbs. tomato paste
3 tbs. flour
2 cups basic stock or chicken stock from which all fat has been removed
1 cup sour cream
2 tbs. fresh parsley, dill or basil, finely chopped

Soak the bread with the light cream in a small bowl.

Heat the bacon fat in a heavy skillet, add onion and cook until transparent. Set aside.

Put into a large bowl the beef, pork and veal. Punch a hole in the center and add eggs, garlic, nutmeg, 2 teaspoons of the salt, ½ teaspoon of the pepper, and the onion, bread and cream mixture. Thoroughly stir and mix with one hand. When completely mixed, form into 1- to 2-inch balls with wet hands.

Add 3 tablespoons of the butter to the skillet in which the onions were cooked, and when foaming, add the meatballs. Cook only one layer at a time, and cook until golden brown all over. Set aside on a plate. Remove this skillet from the heat, and add the remaining salt, pepper, butter, tomato paste, and flour. Mix and add the stock. Cook and stir until thickened.

When thickened, put the meatballs into the sauce, cover, and simmer gently for 20 minutes. Add the sour cream and parsley, dill or basil, and heat. Stir. Do not boil.

To serve: Ladle into a covered, heated serving dish and serve with noodles, rice or steamed potatoes.

Serves 6.

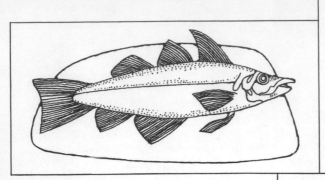

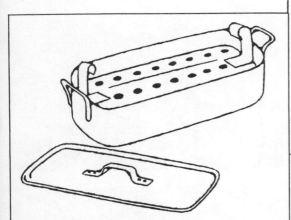

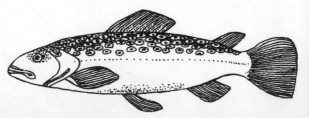

5 *Fish*

FISH NOTES

FROZEN FISH may be substituted for fresh fish with a minimum loss of flavor. However, nothing surpasses the special taste of fish freshly caught from the sea, a mountain stream or a deep, glacier lake.

The stock over which fish is steamed is enriched and can be used again. Pour it into a container and refrigerate or freeze it for future use.

Do not overcook fish.

Bottled clam juice may be substituted for your fish stock, but it's not as good.

All pepper should be freshly ground, and it is preferable to use white peppercorns in fish dishes with a white sauce.

Taste before you serve! Correct the seasoning to *your* taste.

§ FISH ASPIC

Fish aspic does not have as many uses as a meat-base aspic, but it is a real delight, particularly in the summer. If you have a supply on hand you will find it simple to prepare various fish-in-aspic dishes, as well as have the pleasure of chopping it into garnishes for fish salads.

5 cups fish stock
1 medium carrot, scrubbed and coarsely diced
1 medium onion, peeled and coarsely chopped
1 bay leaf
1 lb. fish bones and/or fish heads

4 tbs. unflavored gelatin
½ cup cold water
4 tbs. lemon juice
1 tsp. salt
2 egg whites, beaten to a froth
1 egg shell, crushed

Put the stock, carrot, onion, bay leaf and fish bones and/or fish heads into a large pot. Bring to a rapid boil, and boil uncovered 15 to 20 minutes. Strain into a bowl.

Put the gelatin into a small bowl and add the cold water.

Pour the strained stock into a pot, add the gelatin, lemon juice, salt, egg whites and egg shell. Over heat, beat with a wire whisk until the liquid comes to a boil. Boil for 2 minutes. Remove from the heat, and leave the pot undisturbed for at least 15 minutes.

Gently strain the stock through a fine sieve, pour into a container, cover and place in the refrigerator to set.

This makes approximately 1 quart.

§ FISH IN ASPIC CLARA

The number of calories per serving depends entirely on the amount of sauce served, as the fish itself is without cream or fat.

Once you master the relatively easy process of coating a mold with aspic and adding a few decorations, this dish is simple to prepare. I particularly like to serve the fish, handsomely embedded in watercress and surrounded with lemon slices and capers, for a buffet, or as a first course when the menu includes an especially rich entrée.

This recipe is written in three steps. Each step may be prepared and the result put aside. The final assembly takes only a short time.

STEP 1:

1 whole 4- to 4½-lb. striped bass or trout	2 stalks celery, washed and cut into 1-inch pieces
Cold water	6 sprigs parsley
3 tbs. salt	1 bay leaf
1 carrot, scrubbed and diced	Juice of 1 lemon, or ½ cup dry white wine
1 onion, peeled and finely chopped	1 tsp. salt
	6 peppercorns

Have the fish cleaned, but do not have the head or tail removed: they add flavor to the stock. Wash thoroughly. Put the fish into a large pan, and cover with cold water. Add the 3 tablespoons of salt, and soak for 1 hour. Drain and rinse.

Into a large pot, or fish steamer, put the carrot, onion, celery, parsley, bay leaf, lemon or wine, salt and peppercorns. Place the fish on top, and cover with cold water. Cover and bring to a simmer. Poach the fish at a slow simmer for 25 to 30 minutes, or until it flakes easily when tested with a fork. Remove from the heat, and let the fish cool in the stock.

STEP 2:

Juice of 1 lemon	½ tsp. pepper
1 tsp. salt	

When the stock is cool, remove the fish and discard the head, tail, skin and bones. Strain the stock, and set it aside for the aspic or for future use if you have already made your aspic from a supply of fish stock on hand.

With your hands finely shred the meat of the fish into a mixing bowl. Discard any small bones or pieces of skin. Add lemon juice, salt and pepper. Mix well.

STEP 3:

1 quart fish aspic
   Decorations: Select any combination that pleases your fancy: paper-thin carrot rounds, green or black olives cut into rounds or strips, thin lemon slices, capers, thin truffle slices, thin slices of red pimientos, hard-boiled white of egg cut into rounds or strips
Parsley or watercress

Pour ¼ inch of liquid fish aspic into a 6-up metal mold, either a fish-form mold or a ring mold. Place the mold over a bowl of ice and tilt and turn it until the sides of the mold are evenly coated and the aspic is set. Carefully place your decorations on the set aspic and coat them with another ¼ inch of liquid aspic, then place the mold over the ice until this layer of aspic is set. Add the fish mixture by gently tapping and pressing it into the aspic lined mold. Spoon the balance of the liquid aspic over the fish mixture. Chill in the refrigerator 3 or 4 hours, or until set.

Unmold onto a chilled plate, and garnish with parsley or watercress or any other decorations to your liking. Serve with the following green sauce:

1 cup mayonnaise
1 cup sour cream
½ tsp. Worcestershire sauce
4 tbs. sweet gherkins, finely diced
2 tbs. dill, finely chopped
2 tbs. celery leaves, finely chopped
2 tsps. lemon juice
1 tsp. salt
½ tsp. pepper
½ tsp. prepared mustard

Combine and mix well all the ingredients in a bowl. Chill. Serves 6 to 8.

§ COLD SALMON MOUSSE

A *really wonderful main dish for dinner in the summer, or as a first course in winter. If guests are expected, it can be prepared a day in advance and unmolded and decorated an hour before they arrive. After unmolding, it must be kept in the refrigerator.*

Decorate with capers, lemon slices, hard-boiled eggs, watercress, parsley or chopped fish aspic.

2 lbs. fresh salmon	½ cup sour cream
4 cups cold fish stock	½ tsp. Worcestershire sauce
2 tbs. unflavored gelatin	2 tsps. salt
3 tbs. lemon juice	¼ tsp. pepper
2 tbs. cold water	¾ cup heavy cream
⅓ cup mayonnaise	Vegetable oil

Put the salmon into a large pot, and add the stock. Bring gently to a boil and cover. Simmer for 15 minutes, or until the salmon flakes easily when tested with a fork. Remove the pan from the heat. Allow the salmon to cool in the stock.

When cool, strain the stock and set aside. Remove and discard the skin and bones of the salmon. Break the fish into small pieces and mash with a fork, or put through a blender. Add ½ cup of the strained stock.

Put the gelatin into a small bowl, and soften it with the lemon juice and cold water.

Put 1 cup of the strained stock into a pan and bring to a boil. Add the gelatin and stir until dissolved. Set aside until cool.

When cool, pour into a large mixing bowl and combine with the salmon mixture, mayonnaise, sour cream, Worcestershire sauce, salt and pepper. Mix and blend thoroughly.

Beat the cream until stiff, and fold it into the salmon mixture.

Oil a fish-form mold or a ring mold of 6 cups' capacity, and gently pour the mousse into it. Cover, and put into the refrigerator to set.

When set and ready to serve, unmold the mousse onto a chilled serving platter, garnish and serve with the following cucumber sauce:

1 large cucumber, peeled and seeded	1 tbs. chives, finely chopped
1 cup mayonnaise	1 tbs. lemon juice
1 cup sour cream	½ tsp. salt
½ tsp. prepared mustard	¼ tsp. pepper

Grate the cucumber into a bowl, add all the ingredients and mix thoroughly. Refrigerate and serve in a chilled serving bowl. Serves 6 to 8.

§ FISH PUDDING

A blender is not essential for this splendid dish, but it facilitates the preparation.

Butter	1 small bay leaf
2 tbs. bread crumbs, finely ground	Fish stock
1¼ cups white bread pieces, or 3 hard white rolls	10 tbs. butter
1 cup heavy cream	2 egg yolks
1½ lbs. fish fillets, fresh or frozen	1 cup Parmesan cheese, freshly grated
1 small onion, peeled and sliced	1½ tsps. salt
	Pinch cayenne pepper
	2 egg whites
	3 tbs. butter, melted and browned

Generously butter the inside of a 2-quart metal pudding mold or ring mold, add bread crumbs, place the lid on top and shake vigorously. Discard excess bread crumbs. Set aside.

Soak the bread or rolls in the cream. Set aside.

Put the fish fillets into a pan with the onion and bay leaf; add just enough stock to cover. Place a cover on the pan, and gently simmer 5 to 10 minutes, or until the fish flakes easily when tested with a fork. Discard the bay leaf. Strain the fish over a bowl, and press it firmly to extract as much stock as possible. Save the stock for future use.

If a food chopper is used, put the fish and onion through its finest blade. With your hands, wring the cream from the bread. Reserve the cream, and combine the bread with the fish and onion.

If a blender is used, put the fish, onions, bread and cream into it, and blend until thoroughly mixed.

Cream the butter in a mixing bowl, and add the fish mixture, egg yolks, 3 tablespoons of the Parmesan cheese, salt and cayenne pepper. (Add the reserved cream if the food chopper was used.) Mix well.

Beat the egg whites until stiff, and fold them into the fish mixture. Pour into the prepared mold, cover and steam (see Steaming Directions p. 186) for 1½ hours. If a ring mold is used, cover it tightly with aluminum foil, and tie it with a string.

When ready to serve, unmold the pudding onto a heated serving plate, dribble over it the browned butter, and sprinkle on the balance of the cheese. Serve at once.

Serves 6.

§ *FISH STEW*

This is a thick stew that originated in Peru, where it is known as Chupe de Pescado. Because it freezes, I suggest doubling the recipe; it is a good hearty dish to have on the freezer shelf.

I did not have the good fortune to try this dish in Peru, and I am, therefore, uninformed about the proper etiquette of eating the corn slices. My solution is to pick them up in my fingers, and I suggest my guests do likewise.

2 lbs. fresh or frozen haddock
6 cups fish stock
1 tbs. vegetable oil
1 tbs. olive oil
1 medium onion, peeled and finely chopped
1 medium tomato, peeled, seeded and diced
¼ cup rice
2 medium potatoes, peeled and diced into small cubes

1 tsp. oregano
2 tsps. salt
½ tsp. pepper
½ cup fresh or frozen peas
2 ears fresh or frozen corn cut into thin slices, or 1 cup of canned or frozen kernel corn
½ cup milk
1 egg
¼ cup Parmesan cheese, grated

Poach the haddock in the fish stock until it flakes easily when tested with a fork. Strain the stock into a bowl, and reserve. Shred the haddock, discarding all bones, and set aside.

In a large pot heat the oils, add onion and cook until transparent. Add tomato and rice. Stir and cook until the rice is coated with oil. Heat and add the reserved fish stock. Bring to a boil, and add the potatoes, oregano, salt and pepper. Stir. Cover with a loose-fitting lid, and cook over a low heat until the potatoes are barely tender. Add peas and corn. Cover and cook until tender. Add shredded haddock.

Lightly beat the milk and egg together, and slowly, stirring continuously, pour in a thin stream into the stew. Add the cheese, stir, and bring to a boil. Serve.

To serve: Serve from a heated tureen, or a large heated individual soup plates.

Serves 6.

Variation: Two lbs. of cooked shrimps, deveined and cut into small pieces, can be used instead of haddock.

§ STEAMED COD

Hake may be used instead of cod and is every bit as delicious.

4- to 5-lb. piece of cod	Fish stock
Butter	½ cup dry white wine
½ clove garlic, peeled and cut into thin slivers	

Wash and dry the piece of cod. Rub with butter. Insert the slivers of garlic along the backbone of the fish. Wrap in a layer of cheesecloth.

Pour ½ inch of fish stock into a steamer, add the wine and bring to a boil. Butter the steamer rack, lay the fish on it and place the rack over the liquid. Adjust the heat to a slow boil, place a tight-fitting lid on top and steam for 45 minutes, or until the fish flakes easily when tested with a fork.

In the meantime, prepare the following tomato sauce:

2 tbs. butter
½ lb. mushrooms, coarsely
   chopped
1 tsp. lemon juice
2 cups canned tomatoes

1 tsp. salt
½ tsp. pepper
½ cup heavy cream
2 tbs. parsley, finely chopped

Melt the butter in a sauce pot, and when foaming, add the mushrooms and lemon juice. Stir and cook for 2 minutes. Add tomatoes. Bring to a boil, and simmer for 5 minutes. Add salt and pepper. When ready to serve, add the cream and heat. Do not boil.

To serve: Place the fish on a heated platter, carefully remove the cheesecloth and spoon the sauce over the fish. Garnish with parsley.

Serves 6.

§ STEAMED RED SNAPPER

If your steaming pot is long enough, cook this beautiful fish with its head and tail on. If not, have the head removed, and when the fish is on the platter ready to serve, place an ample bunch of parsley or watercress sprigs in its place.

3- to 3½-lb. red snapper,
   cleaned
1½ cups mushrooms, finely
   chopped
1½ cups shrimps, cooked,
   peeled, deveined and
   chopped into ¼-inch
   pieces
½ tsp. dried basil

3 scallions, including the fresh
   green tops, washed and
   finely chopped
1½ cups cooked rice
1 tsp. salt
½ tsp. pepper
3 tbs. butter
   Fish stock
   Butter
1 lemon, thinly sliced
   Watercress sprigs

Wash and dry the fish.

Put the mushrooms, shrimps, basil, scallions, rice, salt, pepper and butter into a large bowl. Mix. Stuff the fish, and close by sewing with a strong thread, or use skewers. Carefully wrap the fish in 1 layer of cheesecloth.

Pour 1 inch of fish stock into a steamer. Bring to a boil.

Butter the steamer rack, lay the fish on it and place the rack over the boiling stock. The fish should not touch the stock. Adjust the heat to a slow boil, place a tight-fitting lid on top and steam for 40 to 50 minutes, or until the fish flakes easily when tested with a fork.

To serve: Place the fish on a heated serving platter, carefully remove the cheesecloth, and spoon a few tablespoons of the stock over the fish. Garnish with lemon slices and watercress sprigs.

Serves 6.

§ *STEAMED FISH CUSTARD*

An excellent use for leftover fish. However, it is a worthy enough recipe to begin from scratch. Buy approximately 1 pound of any white fish, and poach it. Cooked shrimp, lobster or crabmeat may also be used.

2 cups cooked fish	1 pinch cayenne pepper
2 tbs. dry sherry	8 eggs
¼ tsp. prepared mustard	2½ cups hot fish stock
1 tsp. salt	

Remove all bones and skin from the cooked fish, and flake or shred into small pieces. Add sherry, mustard, salt and pepper.

Place the eggs in a large mixing bowl, and beat them until foamy. Slowly add the fish stock, beating continuously. Stir in the fish mixture, and pour into a 2-quart soufflé dish or an attractive heatproof serving dish. Cover with aluminum foil, and secure the foil tightly around the edges by tying with a string.

Place the dish over 1-inch of boiling water, cover and steam for 50 minutes to 1 hour, or until a knife comes out clean when inserted into the custard.

Serve at once.

Serves 6.

§ FRIDAY'S FILLET OF SOLE

A light, nutritious food, perfect for the family. Buy the finest gray or lemon sole your budget permits. Serve with steamed new potatoes and creamed chopped spinach.

4 fillets of sole, approximately	Salt
½ lb. each	Pepper
Butter	Lemon wedges
¼ cup cold fish stock	

Wash and dry the fillets. Lightly butter each side. Roll the fillets up, keeping the white side on the outside.

Bring 1 inch of water to a boil in the bottom of a double boiler. Butter the top part of the double boiler, and place the rolled fillets in it side by side. Add the fish stock. Put the pot over the boiling water, cover with a tight-fitting lid and cook 8 to 10 minutes, or until the fish flakes easily when tested with a fork.

To serve: With a slotted spoon gently remove the fillets to a heated serving platter, and spoon the juices over them. Lightly sprinkle each fillet with salt and pepper, and garnish with lemon wedges.

Serves 4.

§ CREAMED COD

A quick and easy dish to be served over toast triangles or in a rice ring. The mustard adds a pleasant, piquant touch to the sauce.

4 tbs. butter	1½ cups milk
1 large onion, peeled and finely chopped	1 tsp. salt
	⅛ tsp. cayenne pepper
4 tbs. flour	4 cups cod, cooked and flaked
1 tsp. prepared mustard	½ cup heavy cream
1 cup fish stock	1 tbs. parsley, finely chopped

Melt the butter in a deep, heavy pot, and when foaming, add the onion and cook until transparent. Remove from heat, add flour and mustard. Stir. Add stock, milk, salt and pepper. Return to the heat, stir and bring to a boil. Simmer for 5 minutes. Add cod, stir and simmer for another 5 minutes. Add heavy cream and heat.

To serve: Spoon over toast triangles or into a rice ring. Garnish with the parsley.

Serves 6.

Note: If you are going to serve the cod in a rice ring, cook the rice in fish stock.

§ *FRESH TUNA SAINT RAPHAEL*

A classic Mediterranean dish. The ideal piece of tuna is cut from the center of the fish, near the stomach. Do not buy a piece toward the tail, where the flesh was much too nervous.

If you cannot find the small mushroom caps, use large mushrooms and dice them into small pieces.

2- to 2½-lb. piece fresh tuna	¼ tsp. thyme
2 tbs. butter	1 thin slice lemon
1 tbs. olive oil	1 tsp. salt
2 medium onions, peeled and cut into thick slices	½ tsp. pepper
2 large tomatoes, cut into thick slices	2 tsps. potato flour
	2 tbs. cold water
½ cup cold fish stock	1 pinch sugar
1 small clove garlic, peeled and finely chopped	12 pitted black olives
6 sprigs parsley	12 pitted green olives, unstuffed or stuffed with pimiento
1 bay leaf	12 small mushroom caps

With a knife carefully remove the gray skin on the outside of the tuna.

Heat the butter and oil in a heavy pot, and add the onions. Cook until transparent. Add the tuna, and brown it on both sides. Do not let the onions burn; they should be golden.

Turn the heat down, and place the tomato pieces around the sides and on top of the tuna. Add the fish stock, garlic, parsley, bay leaf, thyme, lemon, salt and pepper. Place a tight-fitting lid on top, and simmer over a low heat for 40 to 50 minutes, or until the fish flakes easily when tested with a fork.

Remove the tuna to a plate, and keep it warm. Remove the tomato skins, bay leaf, parsley and lemon slice.

Dissolve the potato flour in the cold water, and add to the sauce. Turn up the heat, cook and stir until thickened, 3 or 4 minutes. Add the sugar, olives and mushrooms, and cook and stir 5 to 8 minutes. If the tuna has cooled, replace it in the sauce: this dish must be served piping hot.

To serve: Place the tuna on a heated deep platter, spoon the sauce over it and serve at once.

Serves 6.

§ SALMON POACHED IN RED WINE

In cooking, red wine and salmon harmonize beautifully. However, serve this salmon with a chilled dry white wine, not a red. The salmon should be a center cut and in one piece.

3 to 4 lbs. fresh salmon	¼ tsp. chervil
3 tbs. butter	¼ tsp. tarragon
6 leeks, including the fresh green tops, washed and cut into 2-inch slivers	½ tsp. salt
	¼ tsp. pepper
	6 sprigs parsley
1 cup fish stock	Lemon slices
1½ cups dry red burgundy	1 tbs. parsley, finely chopped

Wash and dry the salmon. Melt the butter in a shallow pot, and when foaming, add salmon. Lightly brown it on both sides, then remove it to a plate.

Add the leeks to the pot, and toss and stir until wilted.

Return the salmon to the pot, placing it on top of the leeks. Add the stock, burgundy, chervil, tarragon, salt, pepper and parsley sprigs. Bring to a boil. Adjust the heat to a simmer, cover with a tight-fitting lid and simmer for 35 to 45 minutes, or until the salmon is tender.

To serve: Place the salmon on a heated platter, and keep it warm. Over a high heat reduce the sauce to approximately 1 cup, spoon it over the salmon and garnish with lemon slices and parsley. Serve at once.
Serves 6.

§ *FILLETS OF SOLE LAROQUETTE*

Ask your grocer for the fresh sweet red peppers; they do add an extra touch. However, if they are not available, the canned pimientos make a pleasant substitute. Serve with steamed new potatoes or rice.

4 tbs. butter
2 tsps. lemon juice
½ lb. mushrooms, coarsely chopped
8 scallions, including the green leaves, finely chopped
1 medium sweet red pepper, seeded and diced, or 3 canned pimientos, drained and diced
¾ cup fish stock
½ tsp. salt
¼ tsp. pepper
3 lbs. fillets of sole

Melt the butter in a deep, large skillet, and when foaming, add lemon juice, mushrooms, scallions and red pepper. Stir and cook 3 or 4 minutes; add stock, salt and pepper. Adjust heat to a simmer, cover and simmer for 5 minutes. Add fillets, and cover them with a piece of buttered wax paper. Gently poach the fillets for 8 to 10 minutes, or until they flake easily when tested with a fork.

To serve: Use a spatula to lift the fillets to a heated serving platter. Spoon the sauce over them.
Serves 6.

§ CRAB MEAT AND MUSTARD RING

A *marvelous luncheon dish or first course for a dinner party.*
Serve with crisp rounds of Melba toast and a chilled dry white
wine.
Fresh, canned or frozen cooked crabmeat can be used.

Vegetable oil
4 tsps. unflavored gelatin
2 tbs. cold water
1 cup fish stock
4 tbs. sugar
2½ tbs. dry mustard
1 tbs. butter
1 cup dry white vermouth
2 tsps. lemon juice
1 tsp. salt
Pinch cayenne pepper
½ tsp. paprika
4 eggs
1 cup heavy cream
1 lb. cooked crabmeat
Lemon juice
Watercress sprigs

Lightly oil a 1-quart metal ring mold. Set aside.

Put the gelatin in a small bowl, and cover with the cold water.
Bring the fish stock to a boil; add the gelatin, stir until the gelatin
is dissolved. Remove from the heat, and set aside.

Pour 1 inch of water into the bottom of a double boiler, and
heat. Do not boil. Into the top of the double boiler put the sugar,
mustard, butter, vermouth, 2 teaspoons of lemon juice, salt, cayenne pepper and paprika. Stir until blended. Beat the eggs well,
and stirring continuously, slowly add them to the vermouth mixture. Continue to stir and cook until the mixture is thickened.

When thick, remove from the heat, stir in the gelatin and fish
stock. Chill to the point of setting, but do not set.

When chilled, beat the cream until it is stiff. Fold it into the
mixture with great care; it must be completely blended. Pour into
the ring mold, cover and place in the refrigerator to set.

Remove any pieces of cartilage or shell from the crabmeat, add
a few drops of lemon juice, toss and chill.

To serve: Unmold the ring on a chilled serving plate. Place the
crabmeat in the center, and decorate with watercress sprigs.
Serves 6.

Variation: Cooked, shelled and deveined shrimp can be used instead of crabmeat.

§ CRABMEAT STEW

Use fresh, frozen or canned crabmeat for this recipe. If frozen crab is used, defrost before cooking. Serve with fluffy white rice.

1½ to 2 lbs. crabmeat
½ cup dry sherry
¼ tsp. dried basil
2 tbs. butter
1 medium onion, peeled and finely chopped
1 medium green pepper, seeded, with the white membrane removed, finely diced

3 tbs. flour
2 peeled fresh tomatoes, or 2 canned whole tomatoes, coarsely diced
1½ tsps. salt
½ tsp. pepper
1 small clove garlic, peeled and finely chopped
1 cup fish stock
1 cup heavy cream

Separate the crabmeat, and remove all pieces of cartilage or shell. Pour the sherry over it, add basil, mix, cover and set aside.

Melt the butter in a deep, heavy pot, and when foaming, add onion and green pepper. Stir and cook until the onion is transparent. Remove from heat, add flour, tomatoes, salt, pepper and garlic. Stir and return to heat, and simmer for 5 minutes. Slowly add stock and cream. Cook and stir until the sauce comes to a boil; add the crabmeat, stir and simmer 8 to 10 minutes.

To serve: Serve directly from the pot, or pour into a heated serving dish.

Serves 6.

§ *MUSSELS IN WINE SAUCE*

2 quarts fresh mussels
1 cup fish stock
1½ cups dry white wine
1 bay leaf
2 stalks celery, including the leaves, finely chopped
1 medium onion, peeled and finely sliced
1 carrot, scrubbed and thinly sliced
1½ tsps. salt
6 peppercorns
3 egg yolks
1 tsp. potato flour
2 tbs. brandy
1 pinch cayenne pepper
2 tbs. parsley, finely chopped

Scrub and remove the beards from the mussels. Discard any mussels that are open.

Pour the stock and wine into a large pot, and add the bay leaf, celery, onion, carrot, salt and peppercorns. Add the mussels, cover and bring to a boil. Steam the mussels until they are open, approximately 10 to 15 minutes. Discard any mussels that do not open.

When open, remove the mussels with a slotted spoon to a heated bowl and keep warm. Pour the liquid into a sauce pot through a fine strainer lined with cheesecloth.

Beat the egg yolks lightly in a small bowl, and stir in the potato flour, brandy and pepper. Stirring continuously, pour the egg yolk mixture into the hot, strained liquid. Place over a low heat, or over hot water, and stir and cook until the sauce is thickened. Do not boil.

To serve: Remove the top shells of the mussels, and arrange the mussels in a heated gratin dish or on a deep platter. Pour the sauce over them, garnish with parsley and serve at once.

Serves 6.

§ SHRIMP WITH WINE SAUCE

Here is a quick and delicious dish to prepare if unexpected guests show up, or if just you and your family feel like celebrating with ease. Frozen shrimp are recommended. While they are being defrosted in boiling water, the rice can be cooking and you can make the sauce. Preparation should not take longer than 20 to 25 minutes.

Serve with a tomato and lettuce salad, rolls and a chilled bottle of dry white wine.

1 lb. shrimps, cooked, shelled and deveined, or frozen
3 cups rice cooked in fish stock
6 ozs. sweet butter
½ cup dry white wine
¼ tsp. nutmeg
½ tsp. salt
1 pinch cayenne pepper
4 egg yolks
1½ tbs. brandy
½ tsp. lemon juice
1 tbs. parsley, finely chopped

Combine the cooked shrimp and rice, cover, and keep warm over hot water.

Melt the butter in a double boiler, add the wine, nutmeg, salt and cayenne pepper. Stir.

Beat the egg yolks lightly. Adjust the heat so that the water in the double boiler remains hot but does not boil. With a wire whisk beat the butter mixture and slowly add the egg yolks, in a thread-thin stream. Continue to beat until the sauce is thickened. Add brandy and lemon juice. Stir and cook over the hot water for 1 or 2 minutes. Combine the sauce with the shrimp and rice.

Serve in a heated serving dish, and garnish with chopped parsley.

Serves 6.

6　Vegetables

VEGETABLE NOTES

IT HAS BEEN RUMORED that in Paradise, vegetables are picked at their peak of ripeness, sped to the kitchen and immediately steamed or boiled for a few moments with a pure sweet water. Our world is quite a pace away from Paradise, and the best earthly method to cook vegetables, which, by the time they reach our kitchens, have been out of the garden for days, or more commonly, weeks, is to steam them over, or boil them in, stock.

One of the advantages of steaming vegetables is that a steamed vegetable will not be soggy or get cold while draining. For example, artichokes, which absorb much liquid if boiled and are tedious to drain, can be removed directly from the steamer to the serving plate when tender.

Frozen vegetables should be boiled in, or steamed over, stock instead of water; otherwise, follow the cooking directions given on the package.

The stock in which vegetables are boiled, or over which they are steamed, is enriched by the vegetable. Do not discard it. Return it to your supply of basic stock. However, the stock over which beets and cauliflower are cooked should be kept separate. Suggestions for the use of the beet stock are given in the recipe for steamed beets. The flavor of the stock used to cook cauliflower is too predominant to combine with basic stock; use it in a cauliflower soup, or it can add an interesting flavor to a potato soup.

Steam your vegetables at a slow boil, not at a simmer.

Basic stock, and an alternate classic stock, are given for the stock to use in cooking vegetables. However, any stock you have on hand except fish or ham stock, except where specified, may be used.

Water or canned stock can be used in the cooking of vegetables, but the result will not be as flavorful as it will be if you use your own stock.

All pepper should be freshly ground.

Taste before you serve! Correct the seasoning to *your* taste.

§ ARTICHOKE HEARTS AND CARROTS

This is a recipe your friends will want. Serve it with cocktails, as a first course or as a salad.

12 artichoke hearts, canned or frozen
½ cups olive oil
4 medium carrots, scrubbed and cut into diagonal 1- to 2-inch pieces
¾ cup basic stock or chicken stock from which all fat has been removed
2 tbs. lemon juice
1 tsp. lemon rind, grated
1 scallion, washed, with the root removed
1 tsp. sugar
2 tsps. salt
½ tsp. pepper
1 tbs. parsley, or chives finely chopped

Drain the canned artichokes, or defrost and drain the frozen artichokes. Set aside.

Heat the olive oil in a pot, and when hot, add the carrots. Cover and cook until they are almost tender, about 10 minutes. Add stock, lemon juice, lemon rind, scallion, sugar, salt and pepper. Cook uncovered 4 to 5 minutes.

With a slotted spoon, remove the vegetables. Cool the vegetables and sauce separately.

When cool and ready to serve, remove and discard the scallion and arrange the vegetables on a serving platter. Spoon the sauce over them. Garnish with the parsley or chives and serve.

Serves 4 to 6.

§ BEAN SALAD

Serve as a first course, a salad or even as a main course. The beans can be cooked a day or two in advance.

2 cups dried Great Northern white beans	½ tsp. pepper
	1 tsp. dried basil
1 quart basic stock or chicken stock from which all fat has been removed	½ tsp. thyme
	1 bay leaf
	3 sprigs celery leaves
1½ quarts water	3 sprigs parsley
2 tsps. salt	3 cloves garlic, peeled

DRESSING:

3 tbs. olive oil	¼ tsp. pepper
3 tbs. lemon juice	¼ cup scallions, finely chopped
1 tsp. salt	¼ cup parsley, finely chopped

Soak the beans overnight in cold water to cover. Drain. Put them into a large pot, and cover with the stock and water. Add salt, pepper, basil and thyme. Tie up the bay leaf, celery leaves, parsley and garlic in a cheesecloth bag, and add to the pot. Place a loose-fitting lid on top, and cook slowly for 2 hours, or until the beans are tender. Drain thoroughly into a bowl, and save the stock for future use. Discard the bay leaf, celery, parsley and garlic. Chill the beans 4 hours or overnight.

Approximately an hour before serving, prepare the dressing by thoroughly mixing all the dressing ingredients. Pour the beans into an attractive serving dish, and toss and mix thoroughly with the dressing. Chill until ready to serve.

Serves 6 to 8.

§ RED CABBAGE

8 cups red cabbage, finely
   shredded
1 large apple, peeled and
   sliced
½ tsp. salt
2 cups basic stock or beef
   stock from which all fat
   has been removed

1 medium onion, peeled and
   sliced
1 bay leaf
6 whole black peppercorns
4 cloves
2½ tbs. butter
6 tbs. wine vinegar
6 tbs. sugar

Put the cabbage into a heavy pot, and add apple, salt, stock, and onion. Tie the bay leaf, peppercorns and cloves in cheese-cloth, and add to the pot. Bring to a boil, cover, adjust heat to a simmer and simmer for 1 hour. Add butter, vinegar and sugar. Cover and simmer for 1 hour more.

Serve in individual heated serving dishes.

Serves 6.

§ BOILED CARROTS

8 medium carrots, peeled
1 cup basic stock or chicken
   stock from which all fat
   has been removed

1 tbs. butter
2 tsps. sugar
¼ tsp. salt
1 tbs. parsley, finely chopped

The carrots may be halved, quartered, sliced or cut into strips. Place them together with the stock, butter, sugar and salt into a small, heavy pot. Bring to a boil, cover, adjust heat to a simmer and simmer until the carrots are tender.

When tender, drain off any excess liquid, and save it for the stock pot. Serve in a heated serving dish, and garnish with the parsley.

Serves 6.

Variation: Finely chopped dill, basil or scallion tops may be added instead of parsley.

§ GLAZED CARROTS

3 cups carrots, peeled and sliced	2 tbs. butter
1¼ cups basic stock or chicken stock from which all fat has been removed	2 tsps. sugar
	¼ tsp. salt

Put the carrots and stock into a pot, and bring to a boil. Cover and simmer until the carrots are tender. Remove the lid, and cook until the liquid is absorbed. Add butter, sugar and salt. Toss and stir until the carrots become glazed.
Serves 6.

§ MASHED CARROTS

8 medium carrots, scrubbed and sliced	½ tsp. sugar
2 cups basic stock or chicken stock from which all fat has been removed	½ cup heavy cream
	½ tsp. salt

Put the carrots into a small pot, add stock and sugar. Cover. Bring to a boil, and cook until carrots are tender.

When tender, put the carrots together with the stock through a food mill, or blend in a blender until smooth. Add heavy cream and salt. Return to the pot, heat and serve.
Serves 6.

§ *LIMA BEANS WITH BACON*

6 slices bacon, cut into 1-inch
   pieces
2 shallots, peeled and finely
   chopped
½ medium green pepper,
   seeded, with white membranes removed, and finely
   diced

4 cups cooked lima beans
1 tsp. salt
¼ tsp. pepper
1 cup basic stock or ham stock
   from which all fat has been
   removed

Fry the bacon pieces in a medium skillet until crisp. When crisp, remove with a slotted spoon and reserve.

Discard all but 2 tablespoons of the bacon fat from the skillet. Add the shallots and green pepper. Stir and cook for 3 minutes. Add the lima beans, salt, pepper and stock. Simmer uncovered for 10 minutes, or until most of the stock has been absorbed.

Pour into a heated serving dish, and crumble the bacon over the top. Serve at once.

Serves 6.

§ *MUSHROOMS AND RICE*

3 tbs. butter
1½ tbs. vegetable oil
1 medium onion, peeled and
   finely chopped
1 cup rice
2½ cups basic stock or chicken
   stock from which all fat
   has been removed
1½ tsps. salt

1 tsp. pepper
2 cups mushrooms, including
   the stems, cleaned and
   coarsely chopped
1 tbs. lemon juice
3 tbs. sherry
4 tbs. grated Parmesan cheese
3 tbs. parsley, chopped

Heat 1½ tablespoons of the butter and the oil in a heavy pot. When foaming, add the onion, and cook and stir until transparent. Add the rice, stock, salt and pepper. Stir and bring to a boil. Cover with a tight-fitting lid, turn the heat down to a simmer and cook 30 minutes, or until the liquid is absorbed and the rice is tender.

In another pot melt the remaining 1½ tablespoons of butter, and when foaming, add the mushrooms, lemon juice and sherry. Cook over a high heat for 3 to 4 minutes, tossing and stirring all the while. Pour this mushroom mixture into the cooked rice. Add the cheese, and stir.

Serve in a heated serving dish, and garnish with the parsley. Serves 6.

§ MUSHROOMS STELLA

This recipe is the one exception: it does not use any stock. I include it in this book because it is unusual and delicious. Use the small fresh white mushrooms, about the size of a quarter. If large mushrooms are used, taste will be the same, but they are not as attractive.

The prepared mushrooms can be stored 2 to 3 weeks in a closed container in the refrigerator. They are perfect as a first course or with cocktails.

1 lb. fresh mushrooms	½ tsp. salt
1 tbs. lemon juice	2 scallions, including the green
¾ cup vegetable oil	tops, washed and halved
2 tbs. soy sauce	

Wash the mushrooms in a large pan filled with cold water and to which the lemon juice has been added. Do not remove the stems. Drain, but do not dry. It is important that the mushrooms retain the water they absorbed during the washing process.

Heat the oil in a medium pot, and when hot, add the mushrooms. Toss and turn with a wooden spoon until all are thoroughly coated with oil. Add soy sauce, salt, scallions and stir. Adjust the heat to a simmer, and cook uncovered 20 to 25 minutes, or until the oil has separated from the water.

Remove from the heat and cool. Discard the scallions. Spoon the mushrooms, together with the sauce, into a container and cover tightly. Refrigerate until ready to serve.

To serve: With tongs, or a slotted spoon, remove the mushrooms to a serving plate, or individual plates, and garnish with sprigs of parsley or watercress.

Serves 6 to 8.

§ BOILED ONIONS

24 to 26 small white onions, peeled
½ cup basic stock or chicken stock from which all fat has been removed

2 tbs. butter
½ tsp. salt
¼ tsp. pepper
1 tbs. parsley, finely chopped

Put into a small heavy sauce pot the onions, stock, butter, salt and pepper. Bring to a boil, cover, adjust heat to a simmer and simmer for 30 to 35 minutes, or until the onions are tender.

To serve: Drain off any excess liquid, and save it for the stockpot. Spoon the onions into a heated serving dish, and garnish with parsley.

Serves 6.

§ LARDED POTATOES

If you want a change from boiled, mashed or baked potatoes, try these. They are delicious and go well with any roast. They can be prepared early and reheated prior to serving.

3 tbs. butter
¾ cup salt pork, cubed into ¼-inch pieces
2 medium onions, peeled and coarsely chopped
3 tbs. flour
3 cups hot basic stock or beef stock from which all fat has been removed

2 tsps. salt
1 tsp. pepper
1 small bay leaf
½ tsp. thyme
4 sprigs parsley
6 medium potatoes, peeled and quartered

Melt the butter in a heavy pot, and when hot, add the salt pork and onions. Stir and cook until the pork and onions are crisp and golden brown. Remove with a slotted spoon, and set aside.

Add the flour to the fat in the pot. Stir and cook until light brown. Slowly add the hot stock, stirring continuously. Stir and cook until thickened. Add the salt and pepper. Tie up the bay leaf, thyme and parsley in a cheesecloth, and add to the pot. Stir. Add the potatoes, cover and cook 35 to 40 minutes, or until the potatoes are tender. When tender, add the browned salt pork and onions. Stir.

To serve: Spoon the potatoes and sauce into a heated serving dish. Serves 6.

§ POTATOES AND CREAM

6 to 8 medium potatoes, un-peeled	½ tsp. pepper
1½ tsps. salt	2 tbs. butter
1 cup basic stock or beef stock from which all fat has been removed	½ cup heavy cream
	1 tbs. parsley or chives, finely chopped

Put the potatoes into a pot, cover with boiling water and add ½ teaspoon of the salt. Place a lid on the pot, and cook until the potatoes are barely tender. Drain and peel.

Cut the potatoes into medium slices, and place them in a pot. Add the stock, the remaining salt, the pepper and butter. Bring to a boil, and cook uncovered over a medium heat for 5 minutes. Add the cream, stir and simmer uncovered over a low heat until the potatoes are soft and the sauce is slightly thickened.

To serve: Pour into a heated serving dish, sprinkle with parsley or chives, and serve. Serves 6.

§ RICE RING MARGARET

The vegetables can be prepared early and reheated, or kept hot in a double boiler. The mold of rice can be covered and set into a pan of hot water. It takes but a moment to assemble this unusually attractive and delicious dish. If the artichoke hearts are too large, cut them in half, and if small mushrooms are not available, use thinly sliced mushrooms. The rice is especially tasty if cooked in basic stock or chicken stock.

Butter	8 to 10 artichoke hearts, canned
3 cups cooked rice	or frozen
12 to 14 small white onions,	2 tbs. butter
peeled	¼ lb. small whole mushrooms,
¾ cup basic stock or chicken	including stems
stock from which all fat	1 tsp. lemon juice
has been removed	2 tbs. parsley, finely chopped

Butter an 8-inch-diameter ring mold, and gently pack the rice in it. Cover and set in a pan of hot water.

Put the onions into a small pot with ½ cup of the stock, cover and cook until tender. Drain and set aside.

If canned artichoke hearts are used, drain thoroughly; if frozen artichokes are used, defrost and drain.

Melt the butter in a medium pot, and when foaming, add mushrooms and lemon juice. Toss and cook over a high heat 2 or 3 minutes. Add onions and artichoke hearts. Lower the heat, and add the remaining ¼ cup of stock. Stir and simmer uncovered 5 to 10 minutes.

To serve: Unmold the rice ring on a hot platter, spoon the onions, mushrooms and artichokes into the center of the ring, and garnish with the parsley.

Serves 6.

§ STEWED TOMATOES

2½ cups canned tomatoes
1 cup basic stock or chicken
   stock from which all fat
   has been removed
1 green pepper, finely diced,
   with the seeds and membranes removed

5 scallions, including the fresh
   green tops, finely sliced
4 stalks celery, washed and
   finely diced
1 tsp. salt
½ tsp. pepper
2 tbs. butter

If the canned tomatoes are whole, cut them into 1-inch pieces.
Put the tomatoes, stock, green pepper, scallions, celery, salt and
pepper into a pot, and bring to a boil. Adjust the heat to a simmer,
and simmer uncovered 8 to 10 minutes. Add butter. Stir.

Serve in individual heated bowls.

Serves 6.

§ HOT TOMATO SALAD

3 large tomatoes
6 scallions, including the fresh
   green tops, finely chopped
½ cup parsley, finely chopped
3 medium stalks celery, finely
   diced
½ medium green pepper, finely
   diced, with the seeds and
   white membranes re-
   moved

2½ tbs. fresh dill, finely
   chopped, or 1½ tsps.
   dried dill
½ tsp. salt
¼ tsp. pepper
4 tbs. butter
½ cup basic stock or chicken
   stock from which all fat
   has been removed

Cut a thin slice off the top and bottom of each tomato. Cut
each tomato crosswise, making 2 thick slices. Set aside.

In a bowl mix the scallions, parsley, celery, green pepper, dill,
salt and pepper.

Heat the butter in a large, flat, heavy skillet, and when foaming,
add the tomato slices. Do not overlap. Cover them with the mixed

vegetables, and add the stock. Cover and cook over a medium-high heat 10 minutes.

To serve: With a spatula remove the tomato slices to a heated serving platter or individual heated salad plates, and spoon the vegetables over them. Serve piping hot.

Serves 6.

§ *STEAMED ARTICHOKES*

Artichokes	**Butter**
Lemon	**Salt**
Basic stock or chicken stock from which all fat has been removed	

Prepare 1 artichoke per person. Cut the stem even with the base. Discard any discolored lower leaves. Rinse in a pan of cold water. Drain upside down to remove excess water.

Set the artichoke on its side, and cut ½ inch off the top leaves with a sharp knife. Hold the artichoke upright, and with a pair of scissors snip off the sharp points of the other leaves.

Cut 1 thin lemon slice for each artichoke. Cut each slice into quarters, and stick a piece under the leaves in 4 separate places.

Into a pot large enough to hold the artichokes side by side pour 1 inch of stock. Place a rack, or trivet, over the stock, and set the artichokes upright on it. Place a tight-fitting lid on top, and bring the stock to a boil. Adjust the heat to a slow boil, and steam for 35 to 45 minutes, or until a leaf can be pulled off easily. Save the stock for future use.

To remove the choke, gently push open the center leaves, and with a grapefruit knife, or spoon, remove the hairy choke as well as the small prickly leaves covering it. Reform the artichoke by pressing it firmly together with your hands.

Serve with melted butter to which a few drops of lemon juice and a good pinch of salt have been added, or with a sauce to your liking.

§ STEAMED ASPARAGUS WITH HOLLANDAISE SAUCE

Basic stock or chicken stock from which all fat has been removed

2½ lbs. fresh asparagus, washed and trimmed

Put 1 inch of stock into a large pot or an upright steamer. Place a rack or steam basket over the stock, and place the asparagus in it. Cover with a tight-fitting lid, and bring the stock to a boil. Adjust the heat to a simmer, and steam for 10 to 15 minutes, or until the asparagus is tender.

Remove the asparagus with tongs to a linen towel. Wrap securely; the excess moisture will be absorbed, and the asparagus will stay warm for 10 to 15 minues. Save the stock for future use.

Prepare the following Hollandaise Sauce:

½ lb. butter
4 egg yolks

1 tbs. lemon juice
1 pinch salt

Divide the butter into 3 equal parts. Heat 1 inch of water in the bottom part of a double boiler. Do not let the water boil.

Into the top of the double boil put 1 part of the butter, egg yolks, lemon juice and salt. Place over the hot water, and stir continuously with a whisk, or wooden spoon, until the butter is melted and the mixture is smoothly blended. Add the additional 2 parts of butter, one at a time, and stir each time until the sauce is thick and creamy.

If the sauce is not to be served at once, cover and place in a pan of lukewarm water.

To serve: Arrange the asparagus on a heated serving platter, or heated individual plates, and spoon over them all or part of the Hollandaise.

Serves 4 to 6.

Note: If salted butter is used, do not add additional salt. If a sharper Hollandaise Sauce is desired, add ½ tablespoon more lemon juice.

This recipe makes approximately 2 cups of sauce. 1 to 1½ cups amply serves 4 to 6 people.

§ STEAMED BEETS

I usually cook 2 or 3 extra beets, as they are marvelous cold. Peel and dice them, and add them to a green salad, or slice them and serve as a salad with chopped scallions and a vinaigrette dressing (see p. 178).

6 medium beets	2 tsps. cider vinegar
Basic stock or chicken stock from which all fat has been removed	1 tsp. salt
	½ tsp. pepper
2 tbs. butter	2 tbs. parsley, finely chopped

Cut all but 2 to 3 inches off the tops of the beets. Wash.

Pour 1 inch of stock into a deep pot. Place a rack, or a steam basket, over the stock, and place the beets on or in it. Cover with a tight-fitting lid, and bring the stock to a boil. Adjust the heat to a slow boil, and steam for 25 to 35 minutes, or until the beets are tender when tried with a fork.

When tender, remove the beets, peel and cut into cubes.

Melt the butter in a pan, add beets, vinegar, salt, pepper and parsley. Stir and cook until thoroughly heated.

Serve in a heated serving dish or heated individual side dishes.

Serves 6.

Note: The stock over which the beets were steamed is red and has a strong beet flavor. It should not be used in the stock pot, but it has many uses:

a) When chilled it is jellied and it can be cut into cubes and served cold with a lemon wedge as a first course. This amount will serve 2 to 4.

b) It can be reserved for use in a Winterborscht Soup (see p. 52).

c) An equal amount of basic stock can be added to it, heated and served with a thin slice of lemon on top as a hot beet bouillon.

§ SPICED BEETS

3½ tbs. butter
 2 scallions, including the fresh
     green tops, finely sliced
 3 tbs. wine or cider vinegar
 2 tsps. sugar

 1 tsp. salt
 ½ tsp. pepper
 4 whole cloves
 3 cups cooked steamed beets,
     sliced or diced

Melt the butter in a pot, and when foaming, add the scallions and stir and cook until wilted. Add the vinegar, sugar, salt, pepper, cloves and beets. Stir. Cover and simmer for 10 minutes.

To serve: Remove the cloves, and pour into a heated serving dish. Serves 6.

§ STEAMED CARROTS

Basic stock or beef stock from
    which all fat has been re-
    moved
8 medium carrots, scrubbed
    and halved

 2 tbs. butter
 2 tsps. parsley, finely chopped
 1 tsp. salt
 ½ tsp. pepper

Pour ½ to 1 inch of stock into a deep pot. Place a rack, or steam basket, over the stock, and place the carrots on or in it. Cover with a tight-fitting lid, and bring the stock to a boil. Adjust the heat to a slow boil, and steam for 15 to 18 minutes, or until the carrots are tender.

When tender, put the carrots into a heated serving dish, add the butter, parsley, salt and pepper. Toss and stir until the butter is melted.

Save the stock for future use.

Serves 6.

§ *STEAMED CAULIFLOWER*

Basic stock or chicken stock
   from which all fat has been
   removed
1 medium cauliflower, trimmed
   and washed

½ cup melted butter
1 cup bread crumbs
½ tsp. lemon juice
Salt
Pepper

Pour ½ to 1 inch of stock into a deep pot. Place a rack, or steam basket, over the stock, and put the cauliflower on or in it. Cover with a tight-fitting lid, and bring the stock to a boil. Adjust the heat to a slow boil, and steam for 20 to 30 minutes, or until the cauliflower is tender.

While the cauliflower is cooking, mix the butter, bread crumbs and lemon juice in a small pan, and cook and stir until the bread crumbs are golden.

When the cauliflower is tender, remove it to a hot serving dish, sprinkle with salt and pepper and pour the butter and bread crumb mixture over it.

This stock should be saved for use in cauliflower or potato soup. Serves 4 to 6.

§ *STEAMED GREEN BEANS*

2 lbs. green beans
  Basic stock or chicken stock
    from which all fat has been
    removed

4 tbs. melted butter
2 tsps. salt
½ tsp. pepper
1 tbs. parsley, finely chopped

Cut the ends off the beans and wash. Put 1 inch of stock into a large pot. Place a rack, or steam basket, over the stock, and place the beans on or in it. Place a tight-fitting lid on top, and bring the stock to a boil. Adjust the heat to a slow boil, and steam for 30 to 40 minutes, or until the beans are tender.

When tender, put the beans into a heated serving dish and pour

over them the melted butter, salt, pepper and parsley. Toss. Serve
at once.
  Save the stock for future use.
  Serves 6.

Variation: Wax beans may be substituted for green beans.

§ GREEN BEAN SALAD

3 cups steamed green beans,
  diced into ¼-inch pieces
3 scallions, including the fresh
  green leaves, washed and
  finely chopped

2 medium tomatoes, peeled,
  seeded and cut into thin
  strips
1 tbs. dill or parsley, finely
  chopped

  Mix all the ingredients together in a large bowl, and chill.
Prepare the following vinaigrette:

3 tbs. salad oil
3 tbs. olive oil
1 tbs. vinegar

1 tbs. lemon juice
1 tsp. salt
½ tsp. pepper

  Thoroughly blend all the ingredients, pour the mixture over the
green-bean mixture, toss diligently and serve at once.
  Serves 6.

§ STEAMED LEEKS

12 medium leeks
2 cups basic stock or chicken
  stock from which all fat
  has been removed

¾ cup melted butter
Salt
Pepper

  Cut the tops from the leeks, leaving 2 to 3 inches of light green
leaves. Cut off the roots. Partially slice the leeks lengthwise in
order to wash thoroughly between the leaves to remove all the
sand.

Pour the stock into a pot, and place a rack, or trivet, over it. Place the leeks on the rack, cover with a tight-fitting lid and bring the stock to a boil. Adjust the heat to a simmer, and steam for 15 to 20 minutes, or until the leeks are tender.

When tender, place the leeks on a heated platter and spoon the melted butter over them. Sprinkle with salt and pepper.

Save the stock for future use.

Serves 4 to 6.

Variation: When the leeks are tender, chill and serve with a vinaigrette dressing.

§ STEAMED LIMA BEANS

Basic stock or ham stock
from which all fat has been
removed
4 cups fresh shelled lima beans

2 tbs. butter
1 tsp. salt
½ tsp. pepper

Put ½ to 1 inch of stock into a large pot. Place a steam basket, or rack, over the stock, and put the beans in or on it. Cover with a tight-fitting lid, and bring the stock to a boil. Adjust the heat to a slow boil, and steam for 15 to 18 minutes, or until the beans are tender. Save the stock for future use.

When tender, pour the beans into a heated serving dish, add butter, salt and pepper. Toss and serve.

Serves 6.

§ STEAMED ONIONS

Perfect as a garnish for a roast.

1 cup basic stock or chicken
stock from which all fat
has been removed

24 to 26 small white onions,
peeled
Salt
Pepper

Pour the stock into a deep pot. Place a rack, or steam basket, over the stock, and place the onions on or in it. Cover with a tight-fitting lid, and bring the stock to a boil. Adjust the heat to a slow boil, and steam for 30 to 40 minutes, or until the onions are tender.

When tender, put the onions into a heated serving dish, and spoon 2 tablespoons of the stock over them. Sprinkle with salt and pepper.

Save the stock for future use.

Serves 6 to 8.

§ STEAMED RADISHES

If you have not cooked radishes before, do try now. Serve them as a vegetable with any type of roast or as a first coarse.

30 medium radishes	6 tbs. shallots, or the white part
Basic stock or beef stock from	of scallions, finely chopped
which all fat has been re-	5 tbs. butter
moved	1 tsp. salt
	½ tsp. pepper

Wash radishes, and leave ½ to 1 inch of the green tops un-trimmed.

Put ½ to 1 inch of stock into a heavy pot, add a handful of radish leaves, place a steamer basket, or trivet, over the stock and put the radishes in or on it. Cover with a tight-fitting lid, and bring the stock to a boil. Adjust the heat to a slow boil, and steam for 10 to 15 minutes, or until the radishes are tender.

Melt the butter in a small pan, and when foaming, add the shallots, or scallions, and stir and toss over a high heat for 2 to 3 minutes. Add the tender radishes. Toss and stir for 2 or 3 minutes, and serve at once in a heated serving dish.

Save the stock for future use.

Serves 6.

§ STEAMED SPINACH SOUFFLÉ ERICA

Butter
2 cups cooked fresh or frozen
    spinach, well drained
4 tbs. flour
½ tsp. baking powder
1 tsp. salt
¼ tsp. pepper
1 tsp. lemon juice

½ cup cold basic stock or
    chicken stock from which
    all fat has been removed
4 egg yolks
4 egg whites
½ cup Parmesan cheese, freshly
    grated

Generously butter the inside of a 2-quart metal pudding mold, including the inside of the lid. Set aside.

Put into a blender the spinach, flour, baking powder, salt, pepper, lemon juice, stock and egg yolks. Blend until thoroughly mixed.

Beat the egg whites until stiff, and fold into the spinach mixture. Pour into the prepared mold, cover and steam (see Steaming Directions, p. 186) for 1 hour.

To serve: Turn the soufflé out onto a heated serving plate, sprinkle with the Parmesan cheese and serve at once.

Serves 6.

Note: If you do not have a blender, finely chop fresh or frozen cooked spinach, and beat in all the ingredients except the egg whites, which are folded into the mixture.

§ MEDLEY OF STEAMED VEGETABLES

Basic stock or chicken stock from which all fat has been removed
3 medium carrots, peeled and sliced into thick rounds, or cut into 2- to 3-inch strips
½ lb. string beans, washed, ends removed, and cut into 2-inch pieces

1 small cauliflower, or ½ of a large cauliflower, washed and broken into florets
Salt
Pepper
½ cup hot melted butter
1 tbs. parsley, dill, or chives, finely chopped

Pour ½ to 1 inch of stock into the bottom of a pot. Place a rack, or steam basket, over it. Arrange the carrots, string beans and cauliflower florets into 3 sections on the rack or in the steam basket. Cover with a tight-fitting lid, and bring the stock to a boil. Adjust the heat to a slow boil, and steam the vegetables for 15 to 20 minutes, or until they are tender. Save the stock for future use.

When the vegetables are tender, arrange them in sections on a heated plate or platter, sprinkle with salt and pepper and pour over the hot melted butter. Garnish with the parsley, dill or chives. Serve at once.

Serves 4 to 6.

§ STEAMED NEW POTATOES

Basic stock or chicken stock from which all fat has been removed
18 to 24 small new red or white potatoes, washed

5 tbs. butter
2 tsps. salt
1 tsp. pepper

Pour ½ to 1 inch of stock into a deep pot. Place a rack, or steam basket, over the stock and place the potatoes on or in it. Cover with a tight-fitting lid, and bring the stock to a boil. Adjust the heat to a slow boil, and steam for 25 to 30 minutes, or until the potatoes are tender.

When tender, place the potatoes into a heated serving dish, and toss with the butter, salt and pepper. Serve at once.

Save the stock for future use.

Serves 6.

Note: If you do not enjoy the fresh tender skin of the new potatoes, peel before serving.

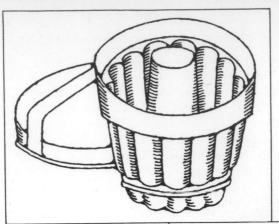

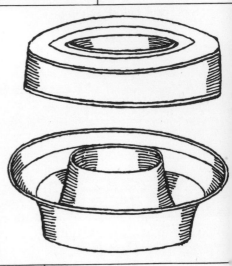

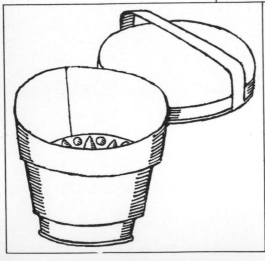

7 Desserts

DESSERT NOTES

A COOKBOOK without a chapter of desserts is like a romantic novel without a happy ending.

In compiling this book of stock recipes, I felt it appropriate to add a few desserts that could be cooked in the stockpot. These are the steamed puddings. Cooking a dessert by steam is much easier than cooking it in the oven. All that is demanded is that sufficient water be in the pot to make the steam. Puddings may be held for an hour or two after the cooking time has elapsed; turn off the heat, leave the mold in the covered steamer, and the pudding will be warm and light when it is unmolded.

Other desserts are included, and except for the Savoy Trifle, they all are prepared on top of the stove.

To whip cream without failure, put a few cubes of ice into a large metal bowl, pour the cream to be whipped into a smaller-size metal bowl, place over the ice, and beat.

STEAMING DIRECTIONS FOR MOLDS

Equipment: Metal molds are used for steaming. These molds are called pudding molds, and are available in various forms. A coffee or lard can, a ring mold or any metal pan can be converted into a mold. If the mold has no cover, cover it with a layer of aluminum foil. The foil should overlap the top by 1 inch and be tied tightly with string. The steam should not seep into the mold.

Molds are available in sizes from ½-cup capacity to 4 quarts. For most recipes in this book, only 1- or 2-quart molds are required.

The rack, or trivet, is the rest on which the mold sits. It may be a trivet, a cake rack, a roasting rack, an opened steam basket or any perforated metal stand. Its legs should be at least ¼ inch in height.

The container for steaming the mold should be a large pot with a secure lid. The lid should not fit tightly, because a small amount of steam should escape. If the pot's lid has an indentation in the center which touches the top of the mold, invert the lid, place it on top of the pot, and place a light weight on it to keep it in place.

Preparation of Mold: The mold should be buttered, sugared or floured according to the directions given in the recipe. It should not be filled more than two-thirds full. A mold of a larger capacity may be substituted for a smaller mold, but remember, never fill a mold to the brim, or part of the ingredients will ooze out into the water.

Steaming: Put 2 to 3 inches of water into the pot. Bring the water to a boil. Adjust the heat to a slow boil. Place the rack or trivet into the pot. It is all right if the water covers the rack and comes up the sides of the mold. Place the mold on the rack; it should sit comfortably inside the pot, leaving space for the steam to flow freely around it. Cover the pot, and steam according to directions.

Note: Two inches of water at a slow boil, in a covered pot, will need 2 to 2½ hours to evaporate. However, it is wise to check the water level once or twice during the steaming time and, if necessary, add additional boiling hot water, since cold water would lower the cooking temperature.

§ STEAMED CHERRY PUDDING

An unusual delicacy that can be served hot or cold. The dark, burgundy-colored juice of the cherries is absorbed into the bread, and when it is unmolded it has an impressive red and white color design.

Butter
Sugar
2½ cups firmly packed white bread cubes
2 cups fresh cherries, halved and pitted, or canned Bing cherries

3 eggs
1 cup sugar if fresh cherries are used; 6 tbs. sugar if Bing cherries are used
1 cup scalded milk
1 tbs. brandy or dark rum

Generously butter and sugar a 2-quart metal pudding mold, including the inside of the lid.

Cut off the crusts of the bread, and cube it into ¼-inch pieces. If canned cherries are used, drain off the juice.

Put a layer of bread cubes into the bottom of the mold, and cover with a layer of cherries. Continue the layers until all the bread and cherries are used. The first and last layers should be of bread.

Lightly beat the eggs and sugar, and slowly add the scalded milk, stirring all the while. Add the brandy or rum. Gently pour this mixture over the layers of bread and cherries. Place the cover on the mold and steam (see Steaming Directions, p. 186) for 1 hour.

To serve: Unmold onto a platter and decorate with sweetened whipped cream sauce (see p. 189), or dribble over it the following raspberry sauce:

1 cup fresh or frozen raspberries
3 tsps. red currant jelly
1 tsp. cornstarch

1 tbs. cold water
½ tsp. lemon juice
1 tbs. kirsch

Mash the raspberries through a sieve so that all the seeds are extracted. Put the purée into a small pot, add the jelly and bring to a boil. Dissolve the cornstarch in the cold water and lemon juice, and add it slowly to the raspberry purée. Stir and cook until thickened. Add the kirsch. This sauce may be served hot or cold.
Serves 6 to 8.

Variation: For the pudding use fresh blueberries instead of the cherries.

§ STEAMED CHOCOLATE PUDDING I

This is delicious hot or cold. Besides being easy to prepare, it is a marvelous way to use up extra egg whites. One of the delights in serving it hot for a party is that it can be made well in advance and left to sit in the steamer for an hour or more after the cooking time has elapsed; it stays warm, and its delicate soufflé quality is not spoiled.

Butter
8 tbs. sugar
8 ozs. semisweet chocolate
2 tbs. apricot jam

8 egg whites
1 tbs. bread crumbs, finely
ground
1 pinch salt

Generously butter a 1-quart metal pudding mold including the inside of the lid; add about 3 tablespoons of the sugar, replace lid and shake vigorously so that the entire surface is coated. Shake out any excess sugar. Set aside.

Melt the chocolate over hot water. Stir. When melted, remove from heat to cool slightly.

Put the jam and 2 of the egg whites into a large bowl, and beat until blended. Add 4 tablespoons of the sugar, and continue to beat until well mixed. Add the bread crumbs and melted chocolate. Mix thoroughly.

Beat the remaining 6 egg whites with the salt. When soft peaks have formed, add the remaining tablespoon of sugar and continue beating until stiff.

Beat 4 tablespoons of the egg whites into the chocolate mixture, and fold the balance in gently. Pour into the prepared mold, cover and steam (see Steaming Directions, p. 186) for 1 hour.

If the pudding is to be served hot, leave the mold in the steamer, with the heat turned off, until serving time. If it is to be served cold, remove from the steamer, cool and refrigerate. Do not remove the pudding from the mold until ready to serve.

When ready to serve, run a knife around the edges of the pudding, and unmold onto a serving plate.

Serves 6.

Serve with the following sweetened whipped cream sauce:

1 cup heavy cream	1 tbs. brandy or dark rum
1 tbs. powdered sugar	

Whip the cream, and when it begins to thicken, add the sugar. Continue to beat until stiff, and fold in the brandy or rum.

§ STEAMED CHOCOLATE PUDDING II

The men in our house say this is the best of all the steamed chocolate puddings. It has a light cake texture, and is a real delight.

Butter	3 tbs. butter
Sugar	2 tbs. flour
1½ cups light cream	5 egg yolks
1-inch vanilla bean, or 1 tsp. vanilla extract	10 tbs. sugar
5 oz. semisweet chocolate, cut into small pieces	2 tbs. dark rum or brandy
	5 egg whites

Generously butter a 1-quart metal pudding mold, including the inside of the lid. Add sugar, place lid on tightly and shake vigorously. Remove the lid, and discard any excess sugar.

Put the cream into a small pot, add vanilla bean, or extract, and chocolate. Place over a low heat, and stir from time to time. Cook until the chocolate is melted. Set aside.

Melt the butter in a small pot, and add the flour. Stir and cook until blended. Slowly, stirring continuously, add the milk and chocolate mixture. Cook and stir until thickened. Remove vanilla bean.

Put the egg yolks and sugar into a mixing bowl. Beat until thick and lemon-colored. Slowly beat in the chocolate mixture. Add the rum or brandy.

Beat the egg whites until stiff. Beat 4 tablespoons of the egg whites into the chocolate mixture. Gently, but thoroughly, fold in the balance of the egg whites. Carefully pour the pudding into the prepared mold, and place the lid on top. Steam (see Steaming Directions, p. 186) for 1 hour.

Prepare the following Sabayon Sauce:

3 egg yolks	2 tbs. brandy or dark rum
3 tbs. sugar	Pinch salt

Put 1 inch of water into the bottom of a double boiler, and bring it to a gentle simmer over a slow fire. Put all the ingredients into the top of the double boiler, and place it over the hot water. With an electric hand beater, or a whisk, beat the mixture until it is thick and holds its shape. To hold the sauce, cover and place it in a shallow pan of lukewarm water.

When ready to serve, turn the pudding out onto a warmed serving platter, and pass the sauce in a sauce dish.

Serves 6 to 8.

Variation: The pudding may be served with sweetened whipped cream sauce, or scoops of vanilla ice cream.

§ STEAMED CHOCOLATE BREAD CRUMB PUDDING

Do you save stale bread or crusts to make crumbs? If you haven't done so, you will want to once you have tried this delectable and easy-to-prepare pudding. It is a fine treat for teen-agers. It can be served hot or cold, and it can be reheated.

Butter	2 eggs
Sugar	1 tbs. butter
3 cups milk	½ tsp. salt
3 ozs. unsweetened chocolate	1 tsp. vanilla extract, or 1 tbs.
1 cup sugar	dark rum
2 cups white bread crumbs	

Generously butter a 2-quart metal pudding mold, including the inside of the lid. Add sugar, place the lid on tightly and shake vigorously; remove the lid and discard any excess sugar. Set aside.

Put 2 cups of the milk and chocolate into a small pot, and bring to a boil. Add the sugar and bread crumbs, and place the pot over hot water. Stir and cook for 10 to 15 minutes until the mixture forms a thick paste.

Beat the eggs slightly in a small bowl, and add the remaining cup of milk and salt. Stir into the chocolate mixture. Add the butter; stir and cook 3 to 4 minutes. Add the vanilla or rum. Pour into the prepared mold, and place the lid on top. Steam (see Steaming Directions, p. 186) for 1 hour.

To serve: Unmold and serve with vanilla ice cream, or sweetened whipped cream sauce (see p. 189).
Serves 6 to 8.

§ STEAMED CHOCOLATE NUT PUDDING

Delicious hot or cold. The nuts should be finely chopped, not powdered. The old-fashioned nut grinder is perfect for this, but a quicker and easier method is the electric blender. If you use a blender, grind only 3 to 4 tablespoons of the nuts at a time at a high speed for 20 to 30 seconds. Do not grind them to a thick, oily paste.

Butter	5 egg yolks
2 tbs. bread crumbs finely ground	4 ozs. almonds, unblanched, finely chopped
4 ozs. semisweet chocolate	½ tsp. baking powder
4 ozs. butter	4 egg whites
½ cup sugar	Pinch salt

Generously butter a 1-quart metal pudding mold, including the inside of the lid. Add bread crumbs, replace lid and shake vigorously. Remove the lid, and discard any excess bread crumbs.

Melt the chocolate over hot water. In a mixing bowl cream the butter and sugar until fluffy. Add the egg yolks, and continue to beat until well blended. Add the chocolate, almonds, baking powder, and mix thoroughly.

Beat the egg whites with the salt until stiff. Beat one-third of them into the chocolate mixture, and gently fold in the balance. Pour the pudding into the prepared mold, cover tightly and steam (see Steaming Directions, p. 186) for 1 hour.

When ready to serve, turn out onto an attractive serving plate, and serve with sweetened whipped cream sauce (see p. 189).

Serves 6.

§ STEAMED FRUIT PUDDING

This is extremely easy to prepare. It is a rich and dramatic dessert for holiday occasions if served with flaming brandy or rum. It can be made a week in advance and reheated over steam prior to serving. The hard sauce can be made 2 or 3 days in advance and stored in the refrigerator.

Butter	1 tsp. lemon peel, finely diced
Flour	⅔ cup brandy or dark rum
¾ cup raisins	½ cup butter
¾ cup apples, peeled and finely diced	¾ cup sugar
	3 eggs
⅓ cup dried apricots, finely diced	¾ cup flour
	½ cup fine bread crumbs
⅓ cup dates, seeded and finely diced	½ tsp. mace
	½ tsp. nutmeg
¼ cup fresh or preserved orange rind, finely diced	¼ cup kidney or beef suet, finely diced

Generously butter a 1-quart metal pudding mold, including the inside of the lid. Add flour, place the lid on top, and shake the mold vigorously. Remove the lid, and discard excess flour.

Put into a bowl the raisins, apples, apricots, dates, orange rind, lemon peel and brandy or rum. Stir and cover. Marinate 6 hours or overnight.

Cream the butter and sugar in a large bowl, and beat in the eggs one at a time. When well mixed, add the flour, bread crumbs, mace, nutmeg and suet. Stir well, and add the marinated fruits, together with the brandy or rum. Stir and pour into the prepared mold. Steam (see Steaming Directions, p. 186) for 3 hours.

Meanwhile, prepare the following hard sauce:

½ cup softened sweet butter	1 pinch salt
2 cups confectioners' sugar	2½ tbs. brandy or dark rum
1 tsp. vanilla	½ cup heavy cream

Put the butter into a large bowl, and cream until fluffy. Gradually work in the sugar. Continue to beat, and when creamy, add the vanilla, salt and brandy or rum. Beat and mix well.

Whip the cream until stiff, and fold it into the butter and sugar mixture. Pour into a serving bowl, cover and refrigerate until set.

To serve: Turn the pudding out onto a heated serving plate, and pass the sauce separately.

Serves 6 to 8.

Variations:

a) A moment before serving heat ¼ cup of brandy or rum, flame and pour over the pudding. Serve at once.

b) Serve with sweetened whipped cream sauce (see p. 189) instead of the hard sauce.

§ STEAMED SCOTCH CHOCOLATE PUDDING

This pudding is to be served hot, and as it is not light in texture, serve small portions and let your guests return for seconds. It has a splendid flavor, and the orange whipped cream sauce complements it perfectly.

Butter	10 egg yolks
Flour	2 tbs. brandy
5 ozs. semisweet chocolate	5 tbs. sifted flour
10 tbs. butter	1 pinch salt
1 cup sugar	

Generously butter a 1-quart metal pudding mold, add flour and place the lid on tightly. Shake vigorously until coated with flour. Discard excess flour.

Melt the chocolate over hot water, and set aside to cool.

Put the butter and sugar into a mixing bowl, and beat until smooth and creamy. Add and beat in 1 egg yolk at a time. Continue to beat until the mixture is fluffy. Add the cooled, melted chocolate slowly, beating continuously. Add the brandy, and fold in the flour and salt. Pour into the prepared mold, and steam (see Steaming Directions, p. 186) for 45 minutes.

To serve: Turn out onto a serving plate, and serve with the following sauce:

ORANGE WHIPPED CREAM SAUCE:

| 1 orange | 4 tsps. confectioners' sugar |
| 1 cup heavy cream | |

Grate the rind of the orange. Whip the cream, and when it starts to thicken, add the sugar. Continue to beat until it is stiff. Fold in the grated orange rind. Serve in a chilled bowl.

Serves 6 to 8.

§ STEAMED RICE PUDDING

A family dessert. The rice can be cooked, and the mold prepared, before shepherding the children to school, and it can be mixed with the eggs and steamed while preparing dinner. Should company show up, dress it up with sweetened whipped cream sauce (see p. 189) and dribble over it a bit of raspberry sauce (see p. 188). We prefer it warm, but it is good cold too.

Eating this rice pudding, you taste the rice kernels. Nothing is mashed, blended or disguised.

6 Graham crackers
1 tbs. sugar
Butter
2 cups cold milk
½ cup Carolina long-grain rice
1 tsp. vanilla, or ½-inch vanilla
bean

½ tsp. salt
4 egg yolks
6 tbs. sugar
1 tsp. lemon juice, strained
4 egg whites

Finely crush the Graham crackers, and mix them with the sugar. Generously butter a 1-quart metal pudding mold and the inside of the top. Add the cracker and sugar mixture, put on the lid and shake and coat all sides as well as the top. Discard any excess.

Put the milk into a pot, and add the rice, vanilla or vanilla bean, and salt. Bring to a boil. Stir. Place a tight-fitting lid on top, adjust the heat to a simmer and simmer for 30 minutes, or until the milk has been absorbed into the rice.

Beat the egg yolks lightly, and add the 6 tablespoons of sugar and lemon juice. Stir into the cooked rice. Beat the egg whites stiff, and fold into the rice mixture.

Pour the pudding into the prepared mold, and steam (see Steaming Directions, p. 186) for 30 to 40 minutes. With the heat turned off, the pudding will stay warm if left in the hot water for 1 to 2 hours.

When ready to serve, turn out onto a plate.
Serves 6.

§ STEAMED VANILLA BREAD PUDDING

Butter
Sugar
4 cups white bread, from which
the crusts have been re-
moved, cut into ¼-inch
cubes

2 cups light cream
2-inch piece vanilla bean,
scraped, or 1½ tsps. vanilla
extract
4 eggs
1 cup sugar

Generously butter a 1½- to 2-quart metal pudding mold, includ-ing the inside of the lid. Add sugar, place the lid on tightly and shake vigorously. Remove the lid, and discard any excess sugar.

Put the bread cubes into the prepared mold.
Scald the cream with the vanilla bean or the extract.
Lightly beat the eggs and sugar. Slowly add the cream to the eggs, beating continuously. Remove the vanilla bean, and pour the mixture over the bread cubes. Place the lid on top, and steam (see Steaming Directions,p. 186) for 1 hour.

To serve: Unmold onto a serving plate and spoon over the pudding a few tablespoons of raspberry sauce (see p. 188). Pass the balance of the sauce in a separate dish.
Serves 6 to 8.

Variation: Instead of the raspberry sauce, serve the pudding with the following hot chocolate sauce:

2 ozs. unsweetened chocolate	1 pinch salt
6 tbs. water	3 tbs. butter
½ cup sugar	1 tbs. brandy or dark rum

Put the chocolate and water into a small, heavy pot, and stir and cook over a low heat until the chocolate is melted. Add sugar and salt. Stir and cook until the sugar is dissolved and the sauce is slightly thickened. Add butter and brandy or rum. Stir, heat and serve.

§ APPLESAUCE PUDDING

If you eliminate the whipped cream, this is a good dessert to serve to weight watchers, since it is relatively low in calories and high in nutriments.

2 lbs. apples	2 tbs. brandy or dark rum
1 thin slice lemon	2 egg whites
Cold water	1 cup heavy cream
½ cup brown sugar	2 tbs. powdered sugar
½ cup white sugar	¼ tsp. nutmeg
3 tbs. butter	¼ tsp. cinnamon
2 egg yolks	

Wash and quarter the apples, and put them into a heavy pot. Add lemon and sufficient water, about ½ inch, to prevent the apples from burning. Bring to a boil, stir, cover with a lid and cook over a medium heat until the apples are soft.

When soft, put the apples through a strainer or food mill. Return the sauce to the pot, and add the sugar and butter. Stir and cook until the sugar is dissolved. Taste for sweetness. If the apples are tart, additional sugar should be added.

Lightly beat the egg yolks with the brandy or rum. Remove the applesauce from the heat, and slowly add 1 cup of it to the egg yolks, beating them all the while. Return this mixture slowly to the hot applesauce, and stir rapidly until well blended. Pour into a mixing bowl and cool.

Beat the egg whites until stiff, and fold them thoroughly into the applesauce. Pour into an attractive glass or crystal serving dish. Chill.

When ready to serve, whip the cream until stiff and add the powdered sugar, nutmeg and cinnamon. Cover the applesauce entirely with the whipped cream, and decorate with a sprinkle of nutmeg.

Serves 6 to 8.

Variation: Add 1 teaspoon of nutmeg and 1 teaspoon of cinnamon to the hot applesauce.

§ *APRICOT MOUSSE*

12 ozs. dried apricots	1½ tbs. dark rum
6 tbs. sugar	3 tbs. almonds, blanched and
1 cup heavy cream	slivered
2 tbs. confectioners' sugar	

Cover the apricots with cold water, and bring to a boil. Adjust the heat to a simmer, and simmer uncovered until the apricots are tender. Add the sugar, stir and cook until the sugar is dissolved. Put the apricots through a food mill, or blend in a blender until smooth. Chill.

Whip ½ cup of the cream until stiff, adding slowly 1 tablespoon of the confectioners' sugar, and the rum. Fold the cream into the apricot purée. Pour into an attractive serving dish, or spoon into individual serving glasses.

Shortly before serving, whip the balance of the cream with the remaining tablespoon of confectioners' sugar until stiff. Spread the cream evenly over the apricot mousse. Sprinkle the almonds over the top.

Serves 6.

§ CHOCOLATE MOUSSE CURTIS

I like the light texture and the strong chocolate flavor of this mousse. Because the whipped cream is folded into the mousse, no last-minute sauce has to be prepared. It is an elegant and easily prepared dessert.

1 tbs. plus 1 tsp. unflavored gelatin	10 tbs. sugar
¾ cup cold water	5 egg whites
6 ozs. semisweet chocolate	1 pinch cream of tartar
1 oz. bitter chocolate	2 tbs. dark rum or brandy
	1 cup heavy cream

Soak the gelatin in ½ cup of the cold water.

Melt the chocolate in a heavy pot over a low heat. When melted, add sugar, gelatin and the remaining ¼ cup of water. Stir and cook until the sugar is dissolved. Remove from the heat, and cool slightly.

Put the egg whites into a large mixing bowl, add cream of tartar and beat until stiff. Beat 3 tablespoons of the egg whites into the chocolate mixture, and gently fold in the balance, together with the rum or brandy.

Whip the cream until stiff, and fold into the mousse.

Pour the mousse into an attractive crystal serving dish, cover and chill until set.

Serves 6 to 8.

§ CREAM VICTORIA

Measure the gelatin carefully so that the cream has the texture of a cream cheese and does not become stiff and rubbery.

Vegetable oil	1-inch piece vanilla bean, or 1
2½ tsps. unflavored gelatin	tsp. vanilla extract
2 tbs. cold water	1 tbs. dark rum or brandy
1 cup heavy cream	1 cup sour cream
½ cup sugar	

Lightly oil a 1½-pint dessert mold, and set aside.

Put the gelatin into a small bowl and soften with the cold water.

Put into a saucepan the heavy cream, sugar and vanilla bean or extract. Place over the heat, and bring to a boil. Stir and cook until the sugar is dissolved. Add the rum or brandy. Remove from the heat, and stir in the sour cream. Mix until thoroughly blended, remove the vanilla bean and pour the mixture into the prepared mold. Cover, and refrigerate until set.

Prepare the following apricot sauce:

1 10-oz. jar apricot jam	2 tbs. dark rum or brandy
2 tbs. water	

Put the jam into a small pot, add water and rum or brandy. Place over the heat, and stirring continuously, bring to a boil. Cook and stir for 2 or 3 minutes. Remove from the heat, and rub the mixture through a fine sieve. Cover and refrigerate.

To serve: Turn the mold out onto an attractive chilled serving plate, spoon half the apricot sauce over it and serve the balance in a side dish.

Serves 6.

Variation: Pile a mound of fresh-washed and hulled strawberries or raspberries in the center or around the mold, and serve with Raspberry Sauce Thérèse (see p. 205).

§ FRUIT COMPOTE

For a really exquisite compote use only the ripest, sweetest fruit in season. The combination of fruit can vary with the seasons and your tastes. The fruit can be prepared early, covered and set to chill in the refrigerator.

The sauce, which I call "fruit stock," can be made and stored in a covered container in the refrigerator for a week or two. It also adds a special touch to a canned fruit compote. However, drain and chill the canned fruit thoroughly before adding the "stock."

4 large oranges	2 medium pears
2 medium grapefruit	1 medium apple
2 medium bananas	1 cup strawberries

Peel the oranges and grapefruit. Remove the skin and seeds from the sections. Peel and score the bananas, and slice into ¼-inch slices. Peel the pears and apple, remove cores and dice into ¼-inch cubes. Wash the strawberries and remove the stems; if the berries are large, cut them in half.

Place all the fruit into an attractive glass serving dish, cover and chill.

Prepare the following "fruit stock":

2 oranges	1 cup sugar
1 lemon	1½ cups cold water

Thinly peel the rind from the oranges and lemon. Remove any of the white membrane from the rind. With a small, sharp knife finely shred the rind into 2- to 3-inch pieces.

Put the sugar and cold water into a small pot, and add the shredded rind. Stir and cook until the liquid boils, adjust the heat to a simmer, and simmer until the rind is translucent.

Remove from the fire, pour into a container, cover and chill.

Just before serving, pour the sauce over the fruit and stir gently. Serves 6 to 8.

Variations:
  a) Add and cook in the sauce 1 inch of fresh ginger, peeled and finely shredded.
  b) Garnish with a few finely shredded mint leaves.
  c) Add 1 cup of defrosted and thoroughly drained raspberries.

§ PEARS IN RED WINE

This recipe may be prepared a week or two in advance. Store the pears in their sauce in the rcfrigerator.

6 medium pears	½ cup sugar
1½ cups dry red wine	1 slice lemon
1 cup water	1 medium stick cinnamon

Thinly peel the pears; do not remove the stems. Core the pears from the underside so that the stems remain intact.

Put the wine, water, sugar, lemon and cinnamon stick into a pot, and bring to a boil. Place the pears into the sauce, adjust the heat to a simmer, cover and poach the pears for 10 minutes, or until just tender, not mushy. If the pears are not completely immersed in the sauce, gently turn them from time to time with a wooden spoon.

When tender, remove the pot from the heat; discard the cinnamon stick and cool the pears in the sauce. When cool, put the pears into a container, pour the sauce over them and chill.

To serve: Put each pear into an individual bowl, and spoon enough sauce over it to cover one-third to one-half the pear.
  Serves 6.

Variation: Apples may be cooked in the same wine sauce. Wash, peel, quarter and remove the core from the apples; cook according to the directions given for the pears.

§ FLOATING ISLAND

The custard can be prepared in advance and chilled. The meringue can be made in the morning and kept in the refrigerator.

3 cups milk

1-inch vanilla bean, or 1 tsp.
vanilla extract

6 egg yolks

1½ cups sugar

Pinch salt

6 egg whites

Pour the milk into a pan, add the vanilla bean or extract, and scald.

Beat the egg yolks with ½ cup of the sugar until lemon color. Pour the milk bit by bit into the egg yolks, stirring continuously. Pour this mixture into a pan or a double boiler, and place over hot water. Cook and stir continuously over a low heat until the custard coats the back of a wooden spoon. This takes about 30 minutes. Remove from the heat, and still stirring, pour the custard into a container. Cover and refrigerate.

To prepare the mold, melt 10 tablespoons of the sugar in a heavy, small cast-iron pan. Stir, and when the sugar is a deep amber color, pour it into a metal ring mold 8 inches in diameter. Turn the mold and coat the bottom, center and sides with the carmelized sugar.

Add the salt to the egg whites, and beat until stiff. When stiff, add the remaining 6 tablespoons of sugar very slowly, beating all the while.

Spoon the egg whites into the prepared mold. Press and tap them down gently so that there are no large air pockets. Place the mold, uncovered, in a pan of simmering water. The water should come halfway up the mold. Simmer for 25 to 30 minutes, or until a knife blade inserted into the whites comes out clean. Remove from the water and cool.

When ready to serve, remove the vanilla bean, and pour the custard into an attractive glass bowl. Be sure the bowl is large enough to hold the meringue. Run a knife around the inner and outer edges of the egg whites, and turn the mold upside down on top of the custard. Allow the liquid carmelized sugar to dribble over the meringue. Discard that which remains in the mold.

Serves 6.

§ COLD BURNT SUGAR SOUFFLÉ

I advise using a metal spoon with a wooden handle to stir the hot melted sugar.

1 tbs. unflavored gelatin	Pinch salt
¼ cup cold water	4 egg whites
¾ cup sugar	1½ cups heavy cream
⅓ cup boiling water	3 tbs. red currant jelly
4 egg yolks	2 tsps. hot water
¼ cup sugar	

Soak the gelatin in the cold water.

Melt the sugar in a heavy cast-iron pot, and cook until golden amber. Stir occasionally. When it is the right color, remove from heat and add the boiling water; stand aside, as the hot sugar will spit and bubble. When the sugar and water are mixed, add the gelatin and return to the heat. Stir for a moment until the gelatin is dissolved.

Beat the egg yolks and the remaining ¼ cup of sugar until light and fluffy. Pour the burnt sugar into a heatproof measuring cup, and slowly, in a fine thin thread, pour it into the egg yolk mixture, beating continuously. (Do not try to pour the sugar into the egg yolks directly from the hot pan, because you would need a heavy hotpot holder to hold the pan and this is too clumsy to control the pouring.)

Add salt to the egg whites, and beat until soft peaks are formed. Beat 2 tablespoons of the egg whites into the yolk and sugar mixture. Gently fold in the balance. Whip until stiff 1 cup of the cream, and fold it in.

Pour the soufflé into a 1½-quart soufflé dish or an attractive serving dish. Cover. Place in the refrigerator until set.

When set, and shortly before serving, put the jelly and hot water into a small pan. Heat and stir until blended. Remove from heat and cool.

Whip the remaining ½ cup of cream, and spread it evenly over the top of the soufflé.

Pour the jelly into a pastry tube or a waxpaper cone. Draw thin

lines of jelly, about ½ inch apart, over the layer of cream. With the back of a dinner knife draw lightly across the jelly lines to from a lattice pattern. Serve at once.
Serves 6 to 8.

§ MIRABELLE FROZEN SOUFFLÉ

A real party dessert. Because it is frozen, it can be made long in advance. It is beautiful to the eye and most pleasing to the taste. It dresses up a simple dinner, or is the grand finale to a sophisticated menu.

The ideal mold for the soufflé is a metal melon mold, but any attractive metal mold may be used.

The liqueur, Mirabelle, is made from a tiny golden yellow plum grown in Europe. If this liqueur is not availaible, substitute brandy or a dark rum.

9 egg yolks
1¼ cups sugar
2 cups heavy cream

½ cup Mirabelle, brandy or
dark rum

Beat the egg yolks until lemon color. Add the sugar bit by bit, and continue beating until the mixture forms ribbons.

Place the egg yolk mixture over hot water; do not let the water boil. Continue to beat until the mixture begins to stick to the side of the bowl and is warm to the touch. I use an electric hand beater for this step. Do not overcook. Remove from the hot water, and continue to beat, slowly adding the Mirabelle, brandy or rum.

Beat the cream until stiff. Beat 2 tablespoons of it into the custard, and gently fold in the balance. Pour the soufflé into a 1-quart metal mold, cover and freeze.

To serve: Turn the soufflé out on a chilled platter. The individual dessert plates should be thoroughly chilled too.
Serves 6.

Variations: Surround the unmolded soufflé with fresh hulled and washed strawberries or raspberries.

§ FROZEN HONEY MOUSSE

As with so many fine recipes, this mousse is simple to prepare. The only step that may demand your full attention is the cooking of the egg yolks and honey. Make a day or a week in advance, and freeze.

I recommend an orange blossom or clover honey for this recipe.

6 egg yolks	3 egg whites
1½ cups honey	1 pint heavy cream
3 tbs. lemon juice, strained	

Put the egg yolks into a mixing bowl, and slowly beat in the honey. Continue beating until the mixture is lemon-colored and fluffy.

Place the egg and honey mixture over hot water; do not let the water boil. Continue to beat with a beater until the mixture is slightly thickened, warm to the touch and begins to show a trace of hardening at the edges. Remove from the hot water, and place over a bowl of cold water or ice. Add the lemon juice, and beat for 2 or 3 minutes. Set aside to cool.

When cool, beat the egg whites until peaks are formed. Fold the whites into the mixture.

Whip the cream until stiff, and fold it into the mixture. Pour into a 2-quart metal mold, and freeze.

To serve: Turn the mousse onto a chilled plate.

Serves 6 to 8.

Variations:

a) Serve the mousse surrounded by fresh washed and hulled strawberries or raspberries.

b) Serve the mousse surrounded by peeled and thinly sliced fresh peaches.

c) Serve the mousse with the following Raspberry Sauce Thérèse:

2 cups fresh or frozen raspberries	½ cup sugar
	2 tbs. kirsch

If frozen raspberries are used, defrost and strain off the juice.

Mash the fresh or defrosted raspberries through a fine sieve to extract all seeds. Pour the raspberry purée into a small pot, add sugar and bring to a boil. Stir and cook until the sugar is dissolved. Add the kirsch, and chill.

Dribble about ¼ cup of the sauce over the mousse, and serve the balance in a sauce dish.

Note: If the frozen raspberries are sweetened, add only 3 tablespoons of sugar.

§ SAVOY TRIFLE

This recipe is the only dessert I've included that requires the use of the oven. It is given because it is my husband's favorite dessert. It is a beautiful combination of cake and a custard cream, a perfect party dish that can be made a day, or even two, in advance.

A tip on preparing the 2 pieces of wax paper on which the cake is turned out: Lap one piece halfway over the other, and secure them together with Scotch tape.

CAKE:

Melted butter	⅔ cup flour
3 eggs at room temperature	1 tsp. baking powder
½ cup sugar	4 tbs. superfine sugar
1 pinch salt	10-oz. jar currant jelly

Preheat the oven at 350° F.

Brush a 11-by-15-inch jelly-roll pan with melted butter. Cover with a strip of wax paper, leaving a 2-inch overlap at each end, and brush with butter.

Into the mixing bowl of an electric mixer put the eggs, sugar and salt. Beat at a high speed until the mixture holds its shape.

Meanwhile measure the flour, add the baking powder and sift twice. When the egg mixture is stiff, sift the flour and baking powder over it, and fold in gently with a rubber spatula.

Spread the mixture evenly on the prepared jelly-roll pan. Place it on the middle shelf of the oven, and bake for 12 minutes.

Remove. Take each end of the overlapping wax paper, and carefully loosen the cake. Dust the top with 2 tablespoons of the superfine sugar. Turn the cake out onto 2 pieces of overlapping wax-paper. Carefully peel off the paper that is now on top of the cake. Sprinkle with the remaining 2 tablespoons of superfine sugar. Roll up tightly in the wax paper, and chill in the refrigerator.

Stir the jelly through a sieve or strainer. When the cake is chilled, carefully unroll and spread the jelly evenly on the top. Roll up again in the wax paper and chill. Prepare the following cream custard:

1½ cups light cream	2 tbs. cold water
1-inch scraped vanilla bean, or	6 egg whites
1 tsp. vanilla extract	2 cups heavy cream
6 egg yolks	2½ tbs. brandy or dark rum
6 tbs. sugar	1 tbs. powdered sugar
1¼ tbs. unflavored gelatin	

Scald the light cream with the vanilla bean or extract.

Put the egg yolks and sugar into a mixing bowl, and beat until light and fluffy. Soak the gelatin in the cold water.

Stirring all the while, slowly mix the egg yolks into the scalded cream. Add the gelatin, and over a low heat, or over hot water, cook and stir until the mixture coats the back of a wooden spoon. Turn into a dish and cool; do not set.

When cool, beat the egg whites until they form soft peaks. Whip 1 cup of the heavy cream until it is stiff. Carefully blend the egg whites into the custard, and gently fold in the cream and 1 tablespoon of the liquor.

Cut enough of the jelly roll into thin slices to line the bottom and sides of a deep glass serving dish. Sprinkle the slices with ½ tablespoon of the liquor. Slowly pour the custard into the dish. Cover, and place in the refrigerator until set. When set, cover the top of the custard with thin slices of the jelly roll. Cover and refrigerate until serving time.

To serve: Whip the remaining cup of heavy cream with the powdered sugar until stiff. Fold in the remaining tablespoon of liquor, and spread evenly over the top of the cake slices.

Serves 6 to 8.

Variation: Instead of covering the top with the whipped cream, put the whipped cream into a pastry bag with a star tube and decorate the top of the trifle with rosettes and fresh strawberries.

Index